The

PREPARED PARENT'S

SENDING YOUR CHILD
TO COLLEGE

OPERATIONAL MANUAL

The
PREPARED PARENT'S
SENDING YOUR CHILD
TO COLLEGE
OPERATIONAL MANUAL

Marie Pinak Carr *and her daughters*

Katharine Carr, Ann Carr & Elizabeth Carr

Dicmar Publishing • Washington, DC

Important Note to the Reader
This book is intended to provide general information, advice and record-keeping
forms for the use of the reader. The contents are believed to be accurate as of the
time of publication. However, the author and the publisher are not engaged in
rendering legal, medical, financial or any other professional services, and the reader
is urged to consult an appropriate professional if any such services are needed. The
reader is also urged to make sure that the contents are applicable to his or her own
needs and accurate at the time the book is consulted. This book is sold without
warranties or guarantees of any kind by the author or the publisher.
All trademarks of third parties mentioned in this book are included for
informational purposes only. This book is not endorsed or sponsored by, or
affiliated with, any of the trademark owners.

by
Marie Pinak Carr
and
Katharine Marie Carr   Emory University 2006;
Georgetown University 2007
Ann Louise Carr   Texas A&M University 2009
Elizabeth Ashby Carr   Boston University 2010

Dicmar Publishing • Washington, DC

Inquiries should be addressed to:
Dicmar Publishing
4057 Highwood Court, NW
Washington, DC 20007
www.dicmar.com

ISBN: 978-0-933165-16-8

All brand-name products cited in this book are
the registered trademark properties of their respective companies.

Printed in the United States of America
First edition

1   2   3   4   5   6   7   8   9

Library of Congress Cataloging-in-Publication Data
Number 2008920846

Dear Parents,

I wish I knew then what I know now. How many times have we all heard this? So much has changed since we were in college; the laws, rules, regulations and in the helpful resources that colleges make available. There are many things that the student needs to do to prepare for college and also a lot that parents need to do and learn before they wave good-bye at the airport or dorm.

Six years and four colleges later, I have tried to keep track of everything we have learned, often the hard way.

What happens when the tuition bill is sent to an email account and ignored?

How can I help when my child gets sick?

How do I manage risks and costs in an expensive time?

A lot happens between being accepted and the first day of class. I hope this book will make the journey easier. My daughters have added chapters, comments and suggestions to help lower the parental anxiety level. Be organized, plan ahead, and make the most of these exciting years.

Sincerely,
Marie Pinak Carr

Contents

BEFORE YOU
EVEN START . . . .

CHAPTER

1

The Best Defense is a Good Offense

Get Organized

▼

CHECKLIST

❏ Create Files

❏ Create Calendar

❏ Receive a copy of your child's class schedule

Save More Money by:

- After comparison shopping, book hotel rooms to lock in the most favorable, lowest price.

- Searching the entire internet for the best airline price and booking with sufficient time to afford you the best price.

- Planning ahead with sufficient time to utilize normal mail and shipping services rather than the expensive next day options.

YOUR CHILD WILL be living independently for the first time and you can expect to receive phone calls about everything and anything.

Once Kate called to ask, "Mom, how do you get spaghetti sauce out of a blouse?"

Ann called when someone hit her car in the parking lot and needed to know how to go about filing an insurance claim.

Beth called asking me if I could retrieve her resumé from the computer or if I had one I could email to her. Another time, she needed to know for the BU Crew Team physical the exact days she had chicken pox in first grade!

Little by little I got more and more organized and now the most unusual request can be answered or handled easily within minutes instead of hours.

CREATE A FILING SYSTEM

- It is imperative that you create a filing system specifically for your child's college and all correspondence and materials related to it.
- Purchase a set of 12 pastel colored hanging files and label them: Bank Accounts, Brochures, College Guide, Credit Information, Correspondence, Housing, Insurance, Maps, Medical, Miscellaneous Travel and Tuition. Should you need to retrieve information from them and you are not at home with your files, it's far easier to tell someone over the phone to find the purple folder marked Medical.
- Inside each folder write the point of contact person and phone numbers.

Make copies of all documents that you give to the college and IMMEDIATELY FILE them. This includes checks and other forms of payments.

CREATE A YEARLY CALENDAR THAT LISTS ...

Move into Dorms/Housing _____

First Day of School _____

Parents Weekend _____

Thanksgiving Vacation _____

First Semester Final Exam Dates _____

Semester Break _____

Second Semester Begins _____

Spring Break _____

Second Semester Final Exam Dates _____

Last Day of School _____

Date Tuition Checks Due–1st Semester _____

Date Tuition Checks Due–2nd Semester _____

Other Important Dates _____

_____

_____

_____

_____

STUDENT'S SCHEDULE

	Monday	Tuesday	Wednesday
8:00 AM			
9:00			
10:00			
11:00			
12:00 PM			
1:00			
2:00			
3:00			
4:00			
5:00			
6:00			
7:00			
8:00			
9:00			
10:00			

STUDENT'S SCHEDULE

Thursday	Friday	Saturday	Sunday

➤ Keep a copy of the student's schedule. If there's an emergency, you will not only know where to reach your child, but possibly which professor needs to be contacted.

➤ If need be, highlight calendar information with a colored marker to distinguish your college bound child's schedule and special dates from others.

TIP

Have your child assist in getting organized. Students need to develop both good organizational skills as well as the ability to prioritize their time to do well in college.

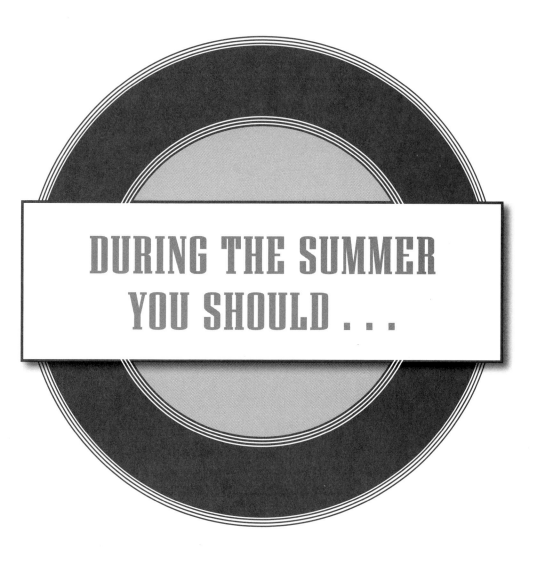

DURING THE SUMMER YOU SHOULD . . .

CHAPTER

2

Paperwork Mountains

Prepare to Climb

▼

CHECKLIST

❑ Health Forms

    Date received _____   Date returned _____

    ❑ Copies filed

❑ Physical Booked

    Date of appointment _____

    ❑ Copies filed

❑ Vaccination Updates

    Date of appointment _____

    ❑ Copies filed

❑ Housing Forms

    Date received _____   Date returned _____

    ❑ Copies filed   ❑ Receipt verified

❑ Tuition Bills

    Date received _____   Date returned _____

    ❑ Copies filed   ❑ Receipts verified

❑ New Student Orientation

    Date received _____   Date returned _____

Save More Money by:

- Not paying for health insurance twice
- Planning ahead with sufficient time to utilize normal mail and shipping services rather than the expensive next day options.
- Having your student monitor their financial student accounts for additional charges. Pay these on time and avoid late charges and interest.

IMPORTANT MAIL FROM YOUR CHILD'S COLLEGE

ONCE YOUR CHILD is accepted and you've sent in your deposit to hold your child's space, you can expect to be bombarded with correspondence and "junk" mail. Everyone will want your child to open an account with them, finance their education through them or purchase from them. Most of these items will be sent to your child who will probably ignore them *(including the **Tuition Bill**)*.

Be on the look out for the following mail items. They will need to be opened and responded to ASAP.

If your child is abroad or out of town make arrangements to have all mail opened and responded to in his/her absence. **DO NOT WAIT** until the end of the summer or the child's return.

Note: each of these topics will be discussed in greater detail in a separate chapter.

HEALTH FORMS

Start gathering all of your child's medical information in one place and **book a doctor's appointment** because your child will most likely need a physical examination and the physician's record of vaccinations and immunizations sent in before school starts. If your child has been recruited to play a team sport you should also be prepared to answer a detailed questionnaire. Beth was recruited to row for Boston University and her questionnaire asked for the exact date that she had chicken pox in first grade.

WARNING

Contact your health insurance company now and determine if your child will be be covered while at college. If so, ask for a separate insurance card in the child's name or a letter stating that you have coverage. (See pages 35 and 41 for additional information.) You'll need this documentation to opt out of any insurance coverage fees that some colleges automatically assess on your tuition bill.

HOUSING INFORMATION

This information could come in a large package containing literature about the housing options, or it could be smaller in nature and direct you to the website for information and sometimes even virtual tours of dorm rooms.

> Fill out the questionnaire and send it along with your deposit as soon as possible. Just as in life, college housing has a pecking order, freshmen are last and it's a "first come, first served" format.

TIP

Often freshmen are housed together in the same dorms and sometimes these dorms are clustered together in the same general area. Within this selection though, there are desired rooms and locations, and these fill up quickly. It's normally a "first come, first served" format and the longer you wait to return your response and deposit, the fewer the options. Regrettably some colleges can not house all of their incoming freshmen and failure to return the form and your deposit in a timely fashion can have the detrimental impact of your child being put on a waiting list, or worse yet, not being housed at all.

In some instances there are "privately owned student residences." In College Station, Texas, for example there is an opportunity to live in either a dormitory setting called the Callaway House or a villas setting called Callaway Villas. Both are walking distance from campus and operated and professionally managed by

American Campus Communities. Rooms in Callaway fill up a full year in advance. These residences have full kitchens, include washers and dryers, and are often a better value than other options.

NEW STUDENT ORIENTATION

All schools offer a first year student orientation. Some schools offer this during the summer and others offer it between the day you move in and the day classes start.

Immediately consult your child and your calendar and then register as soon as possible.

There are always some weekends that are more popular than others.

TUITION BILL

Even though you will probably be paying this, the bill will be directed and mailed to the address your child has provided. Some schools only send electronic invoices to your child's college email account. Many children ignore both the letter and electronic notice and find themselves on campus, excited about the college experience starting, and not able to register for their classes because the tuition was not paid.

> Read the bill carefully, there is often a charge for health insurance that you can opt out of with the proper certifications from your insurance companies.

If the bill is not paid in a timely fashion, your child will not be able to register for classes. "A timely fashion" is determined by the university and not the postmark date on the envelope. In addition, late payments will be assessed a late fee and interest. Always make a copy of the bill along with the method of payment and date. If paying by mail, make sure that you have proof of delivery and plan for its arrival weeks before the due date. Colleges receive thousands, sometimes tens of thousands of tuition checks, and you need your check to be opened and processed before the due date. In addition, there's always the possibility that your payment will get lost in the shuffle or credited to another child.

Your child will be adding charges
through the semester to their "financial
college account."

There will be class course books, activity fees and additional spending money added to their college card. You'll need to stay current in paying these charges and many schools do not send invoices. Ask your child to check the college account several times over the course of the semester. Failure to stay current will result in late fees and sometimes interest charges in addition to your child not being able to register for the next semester's classes.

TIP

➤ Have your child check the account
for confirmation of payment and
registration before heading off to the
campus.

➤ Keep good records—this will facilitate
your ability to correct any errors.

CAUTION

Some colleges and universities are now
combining student identity cards with
ATM cards and check cashing cards.

COLLEGE PAYMENT OPTIONS

Verify the accepted methods of payment. Most universities and colleges accept checks, credit cards and wire transfers.

In case you may need to pay a bill quickly note the following:

- Express Mail Address
- Wire Transfer Information
- Bank
- Bank Address
- Account Number
- ABA Number

ADDITIONAL CORRESPONDENCE YOU'LL RECEIVE

Your child might be asked to submit a photo for a school directory or dorm room bulletin board. Before new students decide to ignore this request they should be reminded that it may seem silly, but failure to do this could mean the only photos missing are theirs.

It'll look like it's official and from the college but . . .

Fraternities and sororities will be sending your child information about their fall rush a period of several weeks in which students, serious about becoming part of the sorority or fraternity life, meet the sisters and brothers and learn about the Greek life and what is expected.

Banks and credit card companies will want you as a customer. Remember, don't limit your selections to the mass mailings of these companies and SHRED the offers you don't want, as many guarantee immediate activation and credit.

Ann just received an unsolicited actual credit card in the mail guaranteeing $6,500 of instant credit. All she had to do was call an 800 number to activate the card. Anyone could have stolen the card, called in, spent the $6,500.00 and she wouldn't have known till the bill arrived 20 days later. In addition, the small print on the back stated that there would be an "activation fee of $199.00, annual fee of $198.00, a rush activation fee of $29.99, late fee of $15.00—and that was before interest charges are added on. So by activating the card she would have been $397.00 in debt before she charged anything and probably not even have known it.

Retailers and other companies will be offering you everything from linens to gift packages to books.

Read the literature and consider the quality of the item before ordering. Often discount prices are low for a reason and similar items can be purchased elsewhere for the same price or less.

Explain to your child that the special, one-time 10% discount **"if they instantly open a store charge card"** can easily be swallowed by the activation fee, yearly maintenance fees or the interest charged on purchases paid for over an extended period of time.

CHAPTER

3

Don't Get
Locked Out
of Health
Care

▼

CHECKLIST

❏ Student ID # _____

❏ Student Health Center at College

   Phone Number _____

❏ Nearest Hospital to College

   Name _____

   Address _____

   _____

   _____

   Phone Number _____

❏ Child's Family Doctor

   Phone Number _____

   Address _____

   _____

   _____

❏ Child's Blood Type _____

❑ Nearest Pharmacy

Phone Number _____

Fax Number _____

Address _____

_____

_____

Name of any prescription(s) being taken and refills available:

_____

_____

_____

_____

_____

❑ Child's Eyeglass Prescription

_____

_____

_____

➤ Plan on transferring any prescriptions before they either expire or run out.

➤ Any special allergies or medical conditions should be discussed.

Save More Money by:

- Downloading and creating your own power of attorney and medical waiver forms.
- Receive free notarization service by going to your local bank with your 2 witnesses.
- Locate a drugstore near your home that also has a store near your child's campus. Plan on giving your child's prescription to the pharmacist at your store and having your child fill and pick up the medications at the store near them.
- Send your child to college with a first aid kit that you have been able to fill with purchases made on sale and at discount stores. When needed, your child won't be dashing to the nearest campus convenience store and purchasing travel size versions at premium prices.

STUDENT HEALTH SERVICES

EVERY COLLEGE AND university has a student health service that is designed to meet your child's health care needs while there. Departments could include everything from medical care, behavioral medicine, crisis intervention counselors to chiropractic and emergency care. Overnight medical care may or may not be an option. Before your child is at college, it is in your best interest to ascertain the scope of their services. In addition, the prepared parent should also know the phone number and address of the nearest hospital and pharmacy.

> Should a true emergency occur, the college will assist your child in obtaining the best care.

TIP

If your child has special needs, you will want to discuss these needs and meet the doctors and nurses ahead of time. Ann has her own set of allergists in College Station along with a pharmacy that fills her prescriptions.

Before your child arrives on campus, every college and university will send you a student information, medical history and physical report form that will need to be completed and returned. Your child will need a physical and a physician's record of immunizations. These forms will require an *"In Case of Emergency Contact"* and also *"Consent of Treatment Permission."* In particular, it's very important to keep a copy of the vaccination record. If your child needs to see someone outside of the university/college medical system, the outside insitution will not, unfortunately, have access to these records—especially the last tetanus shot date.

TIP

Don't forget to ICE your cell phones.

ICE (IN CASE OF EMERGENCY)

Paramedics will turn to a cell phone for clues to a person's identity. Add an entry in the contacts list in your cell phone under **ICE** (In Case of Emergency) with the name and phone number of the person that the emergency services should call on your child's behalf. It only takes a few moments of your time and you can save the paramedics time too. Paramedics know what **ICE** means and they look for it immediately. **ICE** your cell phone *NOW!*

ROUTINE VACCINATION RECORD

Required for all students:

Vaccination	Dose	Date
Diptheria, Pertussis and Tetanus Tdap or Td booster given within the last **10** years		
Hepatitis B *(3 doses required)*	Dose 1	
	Dose 2 *(given 30 days after the first dose)*	
	Dose 3 *(given 4–6 months after the first dose)*	
Measles, Mumps, and Rubella *(2 doses required)*	Dose 1	
	Dose 2	
Varicella *(2 doses required)*	Dose 1	
	Dose 2 *(given 4–8 weeks after the first dose)*	
OR Varicella serological immunity/titer		

Vaccination	Dose	Date
Haemophilus Influenza *(type B)* (optional)		
Hepatitis B		
Polio Vaccination (optional)		
Vaccine Prophylactic (optional)		
Meningitis		
Gardasil (optional for female students)	Dose1	
	Dose 2	
	Dose3	

*The yellow **International Certificate of Vaccination** form is a convenient way to keep track of this information.*

MEDICAL WAIVER INFORMATION

Health Care Proxy

The HIPAA (Health Insurance Portability and Accountability Act) enacted in 1996 requires that all medical information and records be strictly confidential. As a college parent this means two things:

1. You will not be able to voice your opinion to any clinician about your child's medical care.
2. You will not have access to their medical records, x-rays etc.

Individuals over 18 are considered adults and will be expected to voice their own health care decisions and can designate a health care agent to make medical decisions for them in the event that they are unable to make decisions on their own. Each state has its own position on this and some have specific forms that must be downloaded from state websites and filled in.

If your child is sick or hospitalized **you'll need a college/university or state health care proxy on file to direct the medical care** or to be able to speak to the attending physician about the condition of your child.

Your child will need to fill this form out and file it with the appropriate college office and you will need to have an additional copy at home that you can fax to doctors and hospitals.

Power of Attorney and Other Written Consents

Most universities have their own form that they require students to file. Once again this is a form that your child can find in "student accounts" and can download. It is also suggested that you create and have on file a power of attorney. This power of attorney will help you access past medical records should your child need them. Blanket permission is usually not accepted, so permission may need to be granted each time your child wants the provider to discuss care with you.

You can find standard boiler plate power of attorney forms on the web if your college doesn't provide them. Most need to have a notary witness their signing and most colleges provide this service for free. Many banks will also provide this service to their customers, but you'll need to bring your own witnesses.

Ann was stung by a bee, went into respiratory failure and was transported to a hospital via an ambulance. Our power of attorney allowed us to fax the insurance information to the hospital while she was being transported in the ambulance and talk with the emergency room doctors as they treated her. Otherwise, there would have been no communication between us and the treating physicians, and we would have been dependent on her roommates. Unfortunately, the school health proxy was not accessible.

HEALTH INSURANCE

Many states have laws in place that require all full time students to have medical insurance. Sometimes, regardless of your current medical insurance coverage, you will be billed for the insurance offered through the college. If your current insurance will cover your child while away at college, you can usually reject this college insurance and have the charge removed from your bill by filing an insurance waiver form. You may need to submit documentation to support your claim and sometimes all of this has to be done online by your child in their "student link."

It is extremely important that you verify that your insurance will cover your child's medical care away from your home area and in the state that your child will be living as a student. Many out-of-area insurance companies restrict the services they will pay for when you are away from home. It is best to inquire and ask specifically what services are covered by your insurance company prior to coming to campus.

If you have a prescription plan within your insurance coverage, inquire if out of state prescriptions are accepted. If not, you may need to arrange to have the drugs ordered online from a reliable website or be referred to a local physician.

> Fill prescriptions at a drug store that has locations nationwide. This will facilitate retrieving refills in another city.

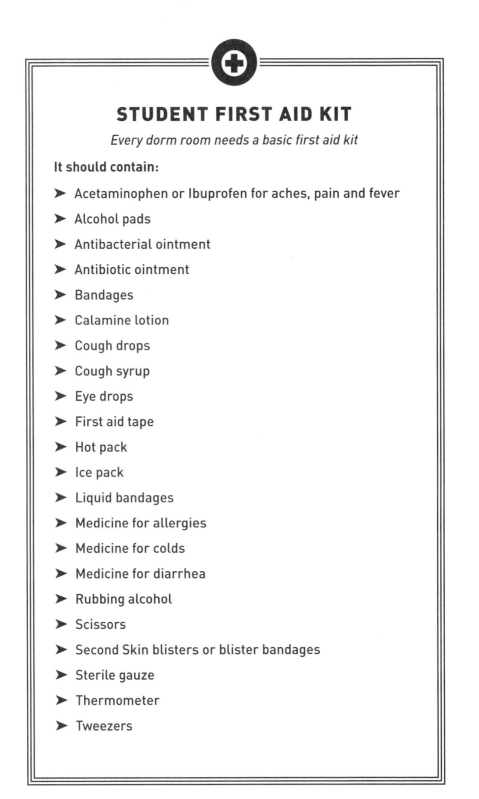

STUDENT FIRST AID KIT

Every dorm room needs a basic first aid kit

It should contain:

➤ Acetaminophen or Ibuprofen for aches, pain and fever

➤ Alcohol pads

➤ Antibacterial ointment

➤ Antibiotic ointment

➤ Bandages

➤ Calamine lotion

➤ Cough drops

➤ Cough syrup

➤ Eye drops

➤ First aid tape

➤ Hot pack

➤ Ice pack

➤ Liquid bandages

➤ Medicine for allergies

➤ Medicine for colds

➤ Medicine for diarrhea

➤ Rubbing alcohol

➤ Scissors

➤ Second Skin blisters or blister bandages

➤ Sterile gauze

➤ Thermometer

➤ Tweezers

HOW TO HANDLE AND TREAT . . .

Determine how to handle and when to treat these as true emergencies and seek immediate medical help:

- Headaches
- Stomach aches
- The common cold
- Cuts and scrapes
- Splinters

- Nosebleeds
- Minor burns
- Ear aches
- Poison Ivy
- Sunburn

One of the most common causes of skin infections is the Staph bacteria.

Health experts advise everyone to:

➤ Frequently wash their hands

➤ Vigorously wash your hand past the wrist

➤ Don't share personal items

➤ Clean and cover with a bandage any cuts or scrapes

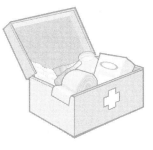

CHAPTER

4

Do You Want to Pay for Insurance Twice?

▼

CHECKLIST

☐ Car Insurance

New Documentation _____

_____

Verified Policy _____

Received _____

☐ Health Insurance

New Documentation _____

_____

Verified Policy _____

Received _____

☐ Homeowner's Insurance

New Documentation _____

_____

Verified Policy _____

Received _____

Save More Money by:
- Not paying health insurance twice
- Making sure out of town prescriptions can be filled without additional costs incurred.

INSURANCES

THERE ARE THREE insurance policies that you need to check and verify the coverage on before your child heads off to college.

Each of these is covered in other sections of this book but bear repeating:

Health Insurance

It is extremely important that you verify that your insurance will cover medical care away from your home area and in the state that your child will be living as a student. Many out-of-area insurance companies restrict the services they will pay for away from home. It is best to inquire and ask specifically what services are covered by your insurance company prior to coming to campus. Ask for a separate insurance card in the child's name or letter stating that the child has coverage.

Many colleges and universities include a health insurance charge as part of a tuition bill. Opt out or you might be paying for insurance twice.

Car Insurance

If your child is taking a car to campus, you will want to check your auto insurance policy. Since the car will be in a new location for at least eight months of the year, this might make a difference in your premiums.

It is important that the company be notified of the new address where the car will be kept. Also inquire about "Good Student" auto-policy discounts for your child.

Homeowner's Insurance

Plan to review your homeowner's insurance policy and its coverage with your insurance agent to ensure that your child will be properly covered while away at college. Inquire if your policy will cover damages and losses due to water, fire, smoke, theft, mold or mechanical break-down.

If your child lives in a dorm or commutes, your homeowner's policy should cover their possessions. Computers, cameras and other expensive items often require an additional personal article rider or floater. If your child has moved off campus, the coverage will cease and you will need to purchase renter's insurance.

Renter's Insurance

There are many companies (that you can find on the internet) that offer insurance to cover your child's possessions while away from home. Usually the landlord's insurance will not cover the replacement value of your child's possessions should the property that your child is renting suffer from smoke, water or fire damage. It is expected that those damages would be protected and covered by a separate policy held by the renter or in this case your child. These policies are affordable, easily transferable from one location to another and the rate depends usually on the value of the possessions, the locations and the size of the rental unit.

Personal Property Inventory

If there is a problem, you will need to file an insurance claim. Before you pack those items to go to college, it's a good idea to take an inventory along with photographs or a video of the higher ticket items. Keep the purchase and warranty receipts and proof of purchases.

On pages 85–87 we have provided more information along with a fill-in chart.

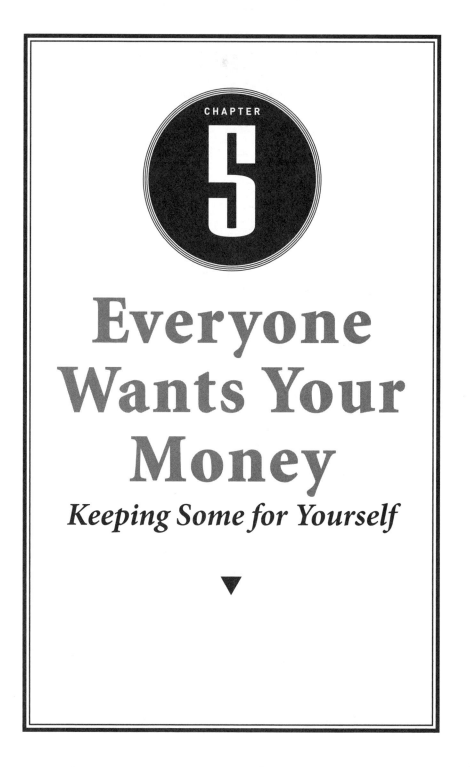

CHAPTER

5

Everyone Wants Your Money

Keeping Some for Yourself

▼

CHECKLIST

❑ Discuss Finances

❑ Make a Budget

❑ Open a Credit Card/Debit Card

❑ Open a Checking Account

  ❑ *Student knows how to write a check*

  ❑ *Student knows how to make a deposit*

  ❑ *Student knows how to keep a register*

  ❑ *Student knows how to reconcile statements*

  ❑ *Discuss with your child the risks of having credit and identity theft.*

Save More Money by:

- Not paying the hidden fees detailed on page 57 such as:
  - ➤ You use another bank's ATM.
  - ➤ Bank balance drops below a certain dollar amount.
  - ➤ You write too many checks.
  - ➤ The credit card company receives your payment one day past the due date.
  - ➤ You overdraw your checking account.
  - ➤ There is an annual card fee.

NOW IS THE perfect time to discuss with your college bound child money management. Open a credit card and/or debit card account in addition to a checking account and make sure your child knows how to write a check, keep a register balanced and reconcile statements. For many children this will be the first time working with a budget.

Help your child get a credit card now before heading off to college, teaching the financial facts that will help your child become a frugal, saving adult who will understand finances and start to establish good credit by opening a savings account, a checking account and paying bills on time. Counsel the student about the high cost of late fees, going over their account limits and bouncing checks.

> ➤ It bears repeating over and over again—
>   SAVE the RECEIPTS

WARNING

➤ If your child is an authorized user on an adult credit card now is a good time to get a credit card in your child's name, and it is often easier to get approved as a student.

➤ Your child will be bombarded with offers of pre-approved credit cards. Compare the offerings and SHRED the offers that you don't want. Never toss these in the trash to become a potential "find" by dumpster diggers who trade on stolen identities.

TIP

Banks provide many different kinds of services. Two are: Bank Accounts and Bank Credit Cards

BANK ACCOUNTS

Checking Accounts

Simply explained, money is deposited into a bank account that allows you to write checks that can be used in lieu of currency for purchases and payments. There are numerous types of checking accounts and often many banking institutions offer special student checking accounts with many advantages including free checks, discounts on purchases and interest on balances.

Before opening a checking account . . .

- Determine the bank services versus the fees

- Determine the convenience of the location of the bank
- Determine the convenience of the bank's hours
- Can you do online banking and if so what are the fees or limitations?
- Is there a limit of checks that you can write each month?
- Is there a required minimum balance?
- Must you direct deposit?
- Is there a limit to teller transactions?
- Does it pay interest on the balance?
- Does it come with a debit or bank card?
- Does it come with an ATM (Automatic Teller Machine) card?
- Does your monthly statement return the cancelled checks to you?
- What are the monthly service charges or maintenance fees?
- Is there a fee per item?
- What is the bounced check charge?
- What is the insufficient funds fee?
- What is the bad check deposit fee (if you deposit a check that bounces)?
- Are there any perks?

➤ Most children pay attention to the free gifts but not the hidden fees.

➤ Most children do not know how to write a check or how to endorse and deposit checks.

➤ It is crucial that you check and balance your checking account and credit card accounts when your statements come in. Any discrepancies should be brought to the bank/card company's attention as soon as possible for resolution.

➤ It's critical that you keep all your receipts and deposit slips in one location so that you'll have them handy to balance your statements when needed.

Savings Accounts

These are accounts in which you deposit your money and earn interest on it. True savings accounts do not let you write checks against the money but rather you need to make withdrawals by visiting either an ATM or bank branch. You may be limited to the number of withdrawals that you can make each month. ATM transactions may or may not be counted as withdrawals.

Before opening a savings account . . .

- Determine the convenience of the location of the bank
- Determine the convenience of the bank's hours
- Determine the convenience of ability to withdraw funds
- What is the interest rate being earned?
- What is the minimum balance required to keep this account?

- How many withdrawals can you make each month?
- How do you make these withdrawals?
- How many ATM transactions can be made each month?

Money Market Accounts

This type of account combines checking and savings into one. Usually you need to keep a fairly high minimum deposit to avoid bank maintenance charges. In return for the higher minimum balance you will be able to earn more interest than a traditional savings or checking account. This is not designed to replace a checking account as you're usually limited to writing five or fewer checks each month.

Before opening a money market account . . .

- Determine the convenience of the location of the bank
- Determine the convenience of the bank's hours
- Determine the convenience of ability to withdraw funds
- What is the interest rate being earned?
- What is the minimum balance required to keep this account?
- How many withdrawals can you make each month?
- How do you make these withdrawals?
- Can you make ATM transactions and if so how many each month?

Certificates of Deposit

Few college students are ready for certificate of deposits (CD), but this is one more piece of the financial picture that your child should at least be aware of. Certificates of deposit are time deposits of money. They are similar to savings and money market accounts in that they are insured and are financial vehicles to earn money on your money. They differ in that you are agreeing up front to a fixed interest rate of return in exchange for leaving your money for a fixed period of time (3 months, 6 months, 9 months, 1 year, 5 years) with the bank or financial institution. Early withdrawal of monies out of a CD usually results in significant financial penalties.

BANK CARDS

There are three different categories of payment cards

- Prepaid cards
- Debit cards
- Credit cards

Prepaid Cards

These are cards with funds already stored in the account and purchases are drawn against that dollar amount. Examples of these are store gift cards. When the funds are used, the cards are no longer good.

Some prepaid cards have activation fees which will lower the available spending power on hand, and some have expiration dates.

Debit Cards

These are cards where a deposit is made in advance and purchases are drawn against this money. This card also doubles as an ATM card allowing for terminal cash-access. Monthly statements show all purchases and ATM activity and are available in a mailed paper format and up to date on-line account information. The account may be replenished with deposits.

> Traditional ATM cards only allow you to
> do transactions at ATM machines.

Debit Cards at a Glance

- Can be used almost everywhere
- Usually only let you spend what you have in the bank, therefore you can't risk charging large amounts that you can't pay for
- Purchases are deducted directly and drawn down against your account's balance from your account
- Pin (personal identification number) based cards add an additional layer of protection against identity theft
- You might be able to charge more than the money you have in the account. This is called "courtesy overdraft"
- Fees will be charged for "courtesy overdrafts"

> Sometimes merchants put blocks on
> your debit card and money. For instance
> if at the local convenience store you
> charge $5.25—you might have a $30.00

block put on your account to guarantee payment. The $30.00 will not be available for your use until the transaction for $5.25 is posted and has cleared. An overdraft fee could be incurred if you purchase with the expectation that you had an additional $24.75 in your account.

My girls have continued to have the credit card issuers and banks use their home address as their official address. They bank and pay charges on-line and don't have to worry about losing or keeping track of the additional paper copies that are sent.

Most cards with free perks have a higher interest rate.

➤ Is your child prepared for responsible spending within a budget?

➤ Keep all your deposit slips and ATM receipts. It's the only way to prove that you have made a deposit or withdrawal.

➤ If you plan to pay in full look for a card with a long period between payment due dates. Some cards will bill you every 25 days, but most are around 20 days.

Credit Cards

These cards allow one to make purchases on a "loan" with the understanding that payments for these purchases will be made sometime in the future. Monthly statements will be mailed, giving you the option of paying in full by the due date or paying a designated minimum amount and having interest charges accrued and added. Current information is also available on line. Credit limits or the maximum amount of charges that you can make are preset on every credit card. If you exceed that amount, your purchase could be denied, a penalty fee can be added to your bill and you may be prohibited from future purchases until your balance is brought down below the limit.

Before opening a credit card account . . .

- Determine if there are any annual fees
- Determine if there are monthly fees
- Is there a fee for cash advances?
- What are the penalties for late payments?
- Is there a charge for point of sale purchases?
- What are the charges for using ATMs out of the plan?
- What are the penalties for account overdraws or exceeding your credit limit?
- Is there a fee for using a PIN number rather than a signature?
- Can you pay online? Most ID theft takes place offline.
- Is there a same day online payment fee?
- What is the interest rate or APR (annual percentage rate)?

- Are there any reward programs that allow you to earn points for transactions?
- Do they reward for good grades and timely payments?
- What is the penalty if the credit card company receives your payment one day past the due date?

TIP

Before leaving for college make two copies of the front and back of your child's driver's license, insurance cards and credit cards. Keep one copy with you at home and the other in a secure place at school.

If the wallet holding these items is ever stolen, all the information will be at your fingertips including the credit card company phone numbers usually located on the back of the cards.

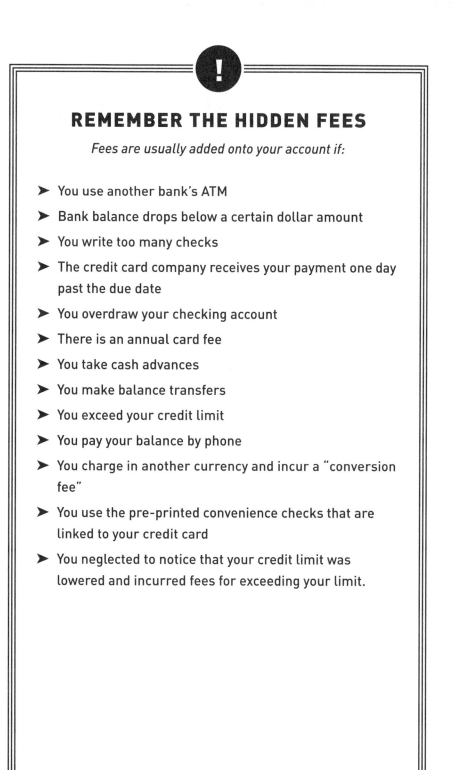

REMEMBER THE HIDDEN FEES

Fees are usually added onto your account if:

➤ You use another bank's ATM

➤ Bank balance drops below a certain dollar amount

➤ You write too many checks

➤ The credit card company receives your payment one day past the due date

➤ You overdraw your checking account

➤ There is an annual card fee

➤ You take cash advances

➤ You make balance transfers

➤ You exceed your credit limit

➤ You pay your balance by phone

➤ You charge in another currency and incur a "conversion fee"

➤ You use the pre-printed convenience checks that are linked to your credit card

➤ You neglected to notice that your credit limit was lowered and incurred fees for exceeding your limit.

TIP

➤ Keep your receipts in a special folder and always check the credit card bill against them. Notify the bank of any discrepancies immediately.

➤ Some good advice when first starting out with credit cards is, if you can't pay it off at the end of the month don't buy it.

➤ Experts favor ATM and debit cards along with checks. Some suggest that a credit card account be opened and available to your child for the bigger ticket items like textbooks, emergency medical care, airfares, car repairs, unexpected emergencies and one-time expenses.

CREDIT SCORE

Once you have a credit card and checking account you'll start to build credit and a credit score. A credit score is based on many factors, two of which are the debt that you have and your history of bill paying. You can get a free credit report every 12 months from each of the three major credit-reporting agencies Experian, Equifax and Transunion through **www.annualcreditreport.com.**

One of the fastest growing areas of identity theft is college students who throw in the dumpster all their solicitations for pre-approved credit cards. Professionals "dumpster dig" for these discarded solicitations and through them can steal your child's identity.

Kate received a notification from her university saying that their student records had been compromised and suggested that everyone obtain a credit report. We were shocked to see all the inquiries from mortgage companies and immediately had her put a fraud alert on.

We also were surprised to see some "late payment notations" made by a retail store. Our daughter had no idea that these payments were late, would be on her credit report for several years and might impact her ability to obtain a car loan or a credit card at a low interest rate.

> **Credit scores change all the time but bad credit history, paying bills late, or not at all can stay with you for years.**

TIP

In brief, your Credit Score is a number based on the following . . .

- About 35% is based on your bill paying history
- About 30% on how much you owe
- About 15% on how long you've had credit
- About 10% on how often you've applied for credit
- About 10% on whether you have credit cards and/or loans

> ➤ Landlords, insurance companies, phone companies, credit card companies and even employers may look at your credit score and use it.

> ➤ When you get your credit report you will not get your credit score.

A credit score and history are extremely important and one should do everything possible to achieve and keep the highest (closest to 850) FISCO score possible. FISCO is the most well know scoring system that uses a value between 300–850 to rate credit.

FINANCING YOUR COLLEGE EDUCATION

College is expensive and, for many, a sacrifice, but the majority of college students today have some form of financial assistance. The best plan is to plan ahead.

FAFSA and CSS

Virtually all colleges and universities require the Free Application for Federal Student Aid (FAFSA) and the PROFILE Financial Aid Application from the College Scholarship Service (CSS) for federal, state and college aid programs. You can look up FAFSA information and forms on line at **fafsa.ed.gov** or call 1-800-433-3243 to speak to someone who can help answer questions or fill out the form. Complete your FAFSA form as early as possible after January 1st of each year.

Types of Aid

There are many different types of grants, loans and work-study programs that you can apply for. The Federal Government sponsors Stafford/Direct Loans, Perkins Loans, Pell Grants, Supplemental Educational Opportunity Grants, Work Study programs and the Federal Family Educational Loan Program. Familiarize yourself with the kinds of assistance available through your high school counselors, by going on line, calling for brochures from the Department of Education or contacting the office of financial aid at colleges you are interested in attending. Counselors will be able to help you understand the type of aid that will be best for you and your student.

Office of Financial Aid

The colleges you are interested in applying to will have an Office of Financial Aid. Contact these people early to find out all of the rules and regulations you will have to comply with to get assistance. Aid funds are typically allocated on a first come first served basis. The college will require specific forms to be filled out and they will have a schedule of deadlines. The earlier you file, the sooner you will find out what your student qualifies for and what your chances of success will be. In addition to grants and scholarships, many colleges have loan and financing options that are unique to the school. Do not assume that all colleges are alike. Many programs differ from state to state. Check out each school you are applying to for their specific aid programs. It may help you make your final decision.

Athletic Scholarships

Some students will qualify for athletic scholarships. Preparing for this opportunity will begin with your high school coach. Talk to the coach about his or her recommendations, the scouting system and the rules of applying for college scholarships. There are strict rules about showing an athlete's capabilities and communicating with future coaches. You must play by the rules to be considered for the opportunity.

Other Loans and Programs

There are other private or semi-private student loan programs and private bank programs using family security. Remember, all loans have a cost and some interest rates are higher than others. Become as well informed as you can, and then make the decision that is best for your student and your family.

FINANCES/STUDENTS
BUDGETING THEIR FINANCES

Budget: Income

List all income available to you from all sources.

One-time income:

Scholarships/Awards	$ _____
Grants	$ _____
Monetary gifts	$ _____
Personal savings	$ _____
Federal Loans	$ _____
Private Loans	$ _____
Other	$ _____
SUBTOTAL ONE-TIME INCOME	$ _____

Monthly income:

Salary/Work Wages	$ _____
Allotment/Allowance	$ _____
Stipend	$ _____
Other	$ _____
SUBTOTAL MONTHLY INCOME	$ _____
TOTAL INCOME	$ _____

One-time expenses per semester:

School related:

Tuition	$ _____
Room	$ _____
Board (Meal Plan)	$ _____
Athletic Pass	$ _____
Books and Supplies	$ _____
Fees	$ _____
Fraternity/Sorority Expenses	$ _____
Lab Fees	$ _____
Parking Permit	$ _____
Transportation (Passes)	$ _____
Other	$ _____

Other one-time expenses:

Cable/Internet Deposit	$ _____
Car Insurance	$ _____
Computers	$ _____
Dorm Supplies/Linens	$ _____
Furniture	$ _____
Health Insurance	$ _____
Renter's Insurance	$ _____
Telephone Deposit	$ _____
SUBTOTAL ONE-TIME EXPENSES	$ _____

Budget: Expenditures

Monthly expenses:

Housing:

Rent $ _____

Cable/Internet $ _____

Newspaper/Magazines $ _____

Telephone $ _____

Utilities $ _____

Other $ _____

Household:

Food $ _____

Dry Cleaning $ _____

Laundry $ _____

Medications $ _____

Toiletries $ _____

Other $ _____

Transportation:

Bus/Subway Fare $ _____

Car Loan $ _____

Car Maintenance $ _____

Gasoline $ _____

Parking $ _____

SUBTOTAL MONTHLY EXPENSES $ _____

Monthly expenses:

Recreation:

Eating Out	$ _____
Entertainment	$ _____
Trips	$ _____
Other	$ _____

Clothing: $ _____

Gifts: $ _____

Monthly Payments:

Credit Cards	$ _____
Membership Dues	$ _____

SUBTOTAL MONTHLY EXPENSES	$ _____
SUBTOTAL MONTHLY EXPENSES *(from page 65)*	$ _____
TOTAL MONTHLY EXPENSES	$ _____
SUBTOTAL ONE-TIME EXPENSES *(from page 64)*	$ _____

TOTAL EXPENSES $ _____

TOTAL INCOME
(from page 63) $ _____

PROTECTING YOUR MONEY
Saving money while living on a budget at college
Don't Impulse Buy

- Buy in bulk—especially snacks and sodas rather than using vending machines.
- Keep track of all ATM withdrawals and plan ahead so as not to have to make several smaller withdrawals in a month.
- Try to microwave and make snacks rather than eating out. Use your meal plan.
- Use your student discount whenever possible.

Watch for Sales and Bargains

- Shop at outlet malls and second hand shops.
- Purchase used textbooks, look at sites such as **www.abebooks.com** and **www.half.ebay.com**
- Let your computer also be your DVD player and multi-task it.
- Leave the car home, you'll save on gas, maintenance and parking, not to mention wear and tear.
- Buy spiral notebooks and other supplies at a local office supply store.
- Make flexible travel plans so you can get the benefits of giving up your seat for a later flight.

Take a personal finance or economic course as an elective.

COMMON SENSE

- Don't leave credit cards or checkbooks in plain view at restaurants, classes or your dorm room.
- Sign cards as soon as you receive them and report any missing ones immediately.
- Memorize your social security and credit card pin numbers. Never write them down.

> 25–35 year olds were most at risk for ID Theft last year.

IDENTITY THEFT

Thieves can access your personal information from:

- Stolen wallets and purses
- Stolen checkbooks
- Stolen credit cards
- Stolen computers
- Stolen mail and pre-approved credit cards that come in the mail
- Stolen insurance cards
- Stolen keychain store membership cards

To reduce the risk of identity theft

- Shred and destroy all pre-approved credit that comes in the mail to you.
- Remove and change any ID that lists your social security number.
- Don't carry any credit cards that you don't need.
- Only purchase online over a secure site.
- Don't print your full name on personal checks, print just your first and middle initial with your last name. (This will increase the difficulty for a thief trying to impersonate you.)
- Don't print your social security number, driver's license or phone number on your check.
- Get and pay bills online.
- Know when to expect your bank statements and bills if they are being sent to your dorm rooms.
- Obtain and review a free credit report annually.

CHAPTER

6

Green is Not Only for Trees

▼

CHECKLIST

❑ Determine dorm needs

❑ Plan ahead and locate items that are recycled and reused

❑ Research and make necessary purchases "green"

Save More Money by:

- Reusing and recycling as much as possible
- Remember the phrase from the Great Depression: "Reuse, rewear, make do and do without."
- Reduce waste especially from phantom electricity draws. Always turn off all electronic devices not in use.

OUR CURRENT ECONOMY presents the perfect excuse for college freshmen to re-use and recycle rather than buy new. You will save time and money and join the movement to go green. With advance planning and conscious, smart choices you can save money and create a "green" dorm room. Rather than purchasing new products that offer style and convenience, opt for gently used items that will be eco-friendly and less expensive.

PLANET AND ECO-FRIENDLY DORM ROOM PURCHASES

1. Search your home. Are there items that you can "re-use" and take to college with you rather than purchasing new? If purchasing, consider looking at used from a local store, Craigslist, Freecycle, etc. With the exception of the mattress, Ann recently furnished her entire apartment for free with discarded furniture from a hotel.

2. Be creative. Can you recycle any items? Desk organizers can be gift boxes, tins and empty plastic food containers. Metal tin cans can be painted and decorated to become attractive holders for pencils, pens, keys, etc.

3. Make smart choices when shopping. Consider packaging material and the miles an item or food has traveled to reach the store. Consider the source of the raw material.

4. Think green. Be conscious of our planet and help preserve our natural resources with your choices.

DORM LIST

Item	Material	Sources
Linens	Bamboo and Organic fibers	
Pillows	Natural Fibers	
Comforters	Organic wool or cotton filled duvet	
Blankets	Organic wool and Organic cotton	
Towels	Organic cotton	
Lamps and Nightlights	Use compact fluorescent bulbs	
Hangars	Bamboo (will last three times longer then wood)	
Show rack	Bamboo	
Sweater Bag	Bamboo	
Storage boxes	Bamboo	
Shoe bags	Partially recycled water bottles	
Drying rack	Bamboo	

Item	Material	Sources
Cleaning Supplies	Use one all purpose or create your own	www.ideabite.com
Furniture	Bamboo	
Clothing	Bamboo	
Messenger Bags	Partially recycled water bottles	www.uncommongoods.com
Plates	Bamboo	
Frying Pan	Bialetti Green Planet Pan uses 50% recycled aluminum and bamboo handles	
Desk Accessories	Bamboo	
Dry Erase Boards	Recycled melamine	
Picture frames	Recycled newspapers	www.target.com
Printer	use all in one printer, scanner, copier	
Paper copies	remember the greenest is no copies at all	
DVD player	use your computer	

SHOPPING GREEN

There are over 94,000,000 results when you Google "shopping green." It really is easier than you think.

➤ Remember to consider the wasteful packaging materials that accompany any purchase and purchase local items. It is said that most food and other items travel thousands of miles to reach the average consumer.

➤ Consider buying in bulk and share with others on your floor.

➤ Bring your own bags and use less plastic. Several groceries stores now give a 5 cent credit per bag that you bring with you.

Eco-friendly Fabrics

- **Bamboo** fibers come the bamboo plant, the world's fastest growing grass. It is 100% biodegradable, breathable, hypoallergenic, highly absorbent and naturally both anti-fungal and anti-bacterial.
- **Hemp** is one of the strongest, natural fibers.
- **Linen** is made from the fibers of the flax plant.
- Organic **cotton** is now an option grown by some farmers without pesticides and from plants that are not genetically modified.

- **Ramie** can be harvested several times a year. It was first used as a cloth in Egypt 7,000 years ago to wrap mummies. It is stronger than cotton or silk, absorbent, has natural stain resisting ability and is anti-bacterial, anti-mildew, and rumored to repel insect attacks. It actually increases in strength when wet.
- **Soy** fibers have the look of silk. They are 100% natural, soft, smooth and lightweight.
- **Tencel** is man made from the cellulose in wood pulp harvested from tree-farmed trees. It is know for its drape. It is soft, breathable and absorbent.
- **Tussah** is a naturally organic silk gathered after the moth emerges. Tussah is generally stronger than other silk threads.
- **Wool** is gathered naturally from goats and sheep.

Green products can be found online and also in:

- Target, Walmart, JC Penny, The Container Store, Bed Bath and Beyond, Crate and Barrel Staples, and others. Consult their web sites for complete listings

Also Consider purchasing:
- Rubbermaid's juice box
- Coffee maker with a thermal carafe style rather than the hot plate coffee makers.
- Plants

- Environmentally friendly non-bleached paper products that contain 100% post-consumer content
- Recycled retractable pens

GREEN CLEANING

Don't use air fresheners. Plan on cleaning your dorm room with Seventh Generation's complete line of non-toxic household products. You can also save money and create your own with vinegar, baking soda, salt and water. Either way you'll be avoiding some potentially volatile organic compounds. See www.ideabite.com for more ideas.

- **Baking soda** can double as a scrub.
- **Vinegar** is considered an acid and therefore will kill many molds, bacteria, and other germs and act as a sanitizer and deodorizer.

Cleaning

Use a mixture of 1 part vinegar to 1 part water for surface cleaning and cleaning mildew. Add more water and you can use it to clean glass.

Add ½ cup vinegar to the cycle rinse of your wash as a fabric softener.

Use vinegar straight up to clean counter tops.

Use a mixture of 1 part baking soda to 2 parts vinegar as a paste to help remove deposits and rings.

Use a mixture of 1 part table salt to one part vinegar as a paste for scrubbing.

Clean your microwave by mixing ½ cup white distilled vinegar and ½ cup water in the microwave.

THINKING GREEN

Reduce, reuse and recycle. Think biodegradable and breathable.

Save energy by:
- Turning off lights when not in use.
- Turning off computers when not in use.
- Turning on printers when a document needs to be printed.
- Be aware of phantom power and unplug chargers when not in use.
- Use fax modems as much as possible.
- Send text messages and emails as much as possible.
- Reduce printing emails and drafts of paper and use both sides of paper. Remember, the greenest paper is no paper at all.
- Boil your own water, use a water filter and fill a reusable bottle.
- Reduce your mail. Always say no to email solicitations or other offers in the mail.
- Take your own snacks and lunch.
- Pay bills on line; it is safer, faster and saves money on postage.
- Instead of purchasing newspapers read them online.
- Remember the greenest paper is no paper at all

TIP

Several states charge you a nickel container deposit. It is refunded after you recycle the plastic bottles and soda cans.

CHAPTER

7

The Dorm Room

A Well-Stocked Locker

▼

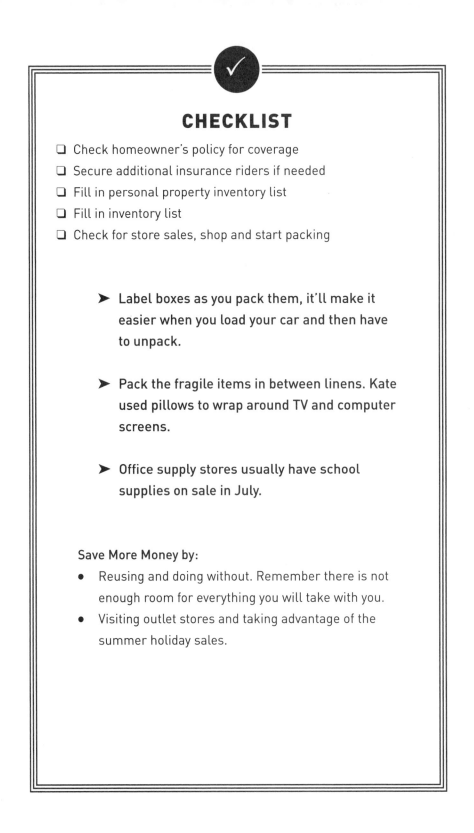

CHECKLIST

- ❏ Check homeowner's policy for coverage
- ❏ Secure additional insurance riders if needed
- ❏ Fill in personal property inventory list
- ❏ Fill in inventory list
- ❏ Check for store sales, shop and start packing

➤ Label boxes as you pack them, it'll make it easier when you load your car and then have to unpack.

➤ Pack the fragile items in between linens. Kate used pillows to wrap around TV and computer screens.

➤ Office supply stores usually have school supplies on sale in July.

Save More Money by:

- Reusing and doing without. Remember there is not enough room for everything you will take with you.
- Visiting outlet stores and taking advantage of the summer holiday sales.

INSURANCE/RENTER'S INSURANCE

EVERY YEAR COLLEGE students bring with them to college $5,000–$10,000 dollars worth of bicycles, stereo equipment, televisions, computers, books, cameras and other personal property that are at risk for damage or loss from fire, water, vandalism and theft.

Plan to review your homeowner's insurance policy and its coverage with your insurance agent to ensure that your child will be properly covered while away at college. If your child lives in a dorm or commutes, your homeowner's policy should cover his or her possessions. Computers, cameras and other expensive items often require an additional personal article rider or floater. If your child has moved off campus, the coverage will be ended and you will need to purchase renter's insurance.

WHAT SHOULD YOUR CHILD TAKE

Before you pack the refrigerator, carpet, or TV **talk with next year's roommate**. In most dorm rooms space is extremely limited and some halls do not have any additional storage space other than closets within the room. It is best to bring only what you need and to postpone purchases of any shared items until after you arrive.

PERSONAL PROPERTY INVENTORY

Before you pack those items to go to college, it's a good idea to take an inventory along with photographs or a video of the higher ticket items.

In addition this inventory should include purchase receipts along with the model and serial numbers. Any warranty information should also be listed. This could help in recovering stolen or damaged property.

Use the inventory lists on pages 85–87 to record your posessions and their warranty.

PERSONAL PROPERTY INVENTORY CHECKLIST

Items	$ Value
Bicycle	
Camera	
Cell Phone	
Clothes/Shoes/Purses	
Computers and Printers	
Electrical Items (DVD Player, Ipod, Radio, Stereo, TV, etc)	
Furniture	
Jewelry	
Linens	
Musical Instruments	
Photo/Film Gear	
Sports Equipment	
Textbooks	
Other	
Add $1,000 for unlisted items	$1,000
TOTAL	

PERSONAL PROPERTY INFORMATION

Item	Description	Model #
Bicycle		
Camera		
Cell Phone		
Computer & Peripheral Equipment		
iPod		
Musical Instrument		
Stereo/ DVD		
TV		
Other		

Purchase Serial #	Warranty Date	Expires	$ Value

TIP

➤ Be advised that many residence hall beds have extended length mattresses and standard size bedding does not fit them. Some dorms now offer double size beds.

➤ Create a special box or tin where your child will always put keys, wallet, sunglasses, glasses and other essential items in daily use.

➤ Save space by rotating clothing. Plan on bringing home your summer clothing and taking back your winter clothing at Thanksgiving break. You can bring those summer items back to school and return the winter items after spring break. Parents Weekend is another good time to swap clothing and other items.

➤ Rugs are readily available for purchase in stores near campuses. I have always bought a rug. It adds another layer of cushioning, keeps the dust down, is cleaner than the existing floor or carpet and adds some color to a plain dorm room.

The following is a list containing almost everything that you could think of to bring. Use it as a guide and once again plan on taking only what you need. **REMEMBER whatever you take will have to either be stored or come back home with you at the end of the semester.**

FURNISHING A DORM ROOM

Linens

- 2 extra-long sheet sets (flat sheet, fitted sheet and 2 pillow cases)
- 1 extra-long mattress pad (mattress dimension is 36" × 6" × 80")
- 1 extra-long egg crate pad or fiberbed/ featherbed to soften an uncomfortable mattress
- 1 comforter (washable since you'll spend most of your time on it)
- 2 pillows
- 1 fleece blanket (can purchase at school)
- 2 bath sheets (extra large towels)
- 1 hand towel
- 1 wash cloth

Room, Closet and Storage

- Bed lifts or rack raisers
- Bookcase/shelving unit
- Clear plastic boxes
- Collapsible folding crate
- Door mirror
- Drawer liners/shelf paper
- Drawer organizers
- Extension cords
- Floor lamps
- Hangers and add-on multiple hangers
- Jewelry organizer
- Night light
- Over-door hooks
- "S" hooks

- Table lamps
- Under-bed drawers

TIP

Usually you have 3–4 dresser drawers and a reasonable size closet. You may want to raise the bed and utilize the space underneath for additional storage.

Cleaning/Laundry

- Broom & dust pan
- Cleaning supplies
- Clothes hamper
- Drying rack
- Goo Gone
- Iron and portable ironing board (optional—most students will never use)
- Laundry basket with name on it
- Lint brush
- Paper towels, tissues, etc.
- Portable vacuum cleaner
- Stain remover
- Wrinkle-free spray

Eating/Cooking

- Airtight food storage containers
- Bowls
- Can/bottle opener
- Chip clips
- Coffee/travel mugs
- Cups
- Ice cube trays
- Magnetic paper towel holder and paper towels

- Microfridge (microwave/refrigerator combo)
- Microwave-safe food containers
- Plates
- Quart size plastic bags
- Salt and pepper shakers
- Silverware
- Water filtering pitcher and replacement filters

> ➤ For your late night snacks you'll want
> to have on hand a supply of packages
> of sugar, sweeteners, ketchup,
> mayonnaise and mustard that you can
> usually find at fast food establishments.

> ➤ Freezer paper (found a grocery store)
> or recycled wrapping paper make
> wonderful, cost-effective means of
> lining drawers and shelves.

TIP

Electronics
- All in one printer/scanner/copier
- Backup software
- Batteries
- Cable cord
- CD-Rs
- Computer (college may offer discounts)
- Computer screen (unless you have a laptop)
- Digital camera
- DVD player
- Ethernet cord
- Extension cord
- Inkjet cartridges

- Jump drive
- Mouse pad
- MP3 player
- Power strip/surge protector
- Television
- Wireless card

Must Haves
- Alarm clock/clock radio
- Cell phone
- Compact umbrella
- Duffle/overnight bag
- Fan
- First aid kit (see page 36)

Sewing Kit
- Pins
- Buttons
- Thread
- Sewing needles

➤ There are some wonderful hotel sewing kits that contain almost everything that your child will need and already have the needles threaded with various colored threads.

➤ Chances are that your child will not be mending anything but every now and then a button falls off that will need to be replaced. Remember that dry cleaners often can mend and hem for a nominal charge.

Showering

- Bath robe
- Cosmetics & toiletries
- Flip flops or Crocs
- Hair dryer
- Mirror
- Over-door towel rack
- Plastic cup
- Soap container
- Toiletries
- Toothbrush holder
- Waterproof shower caddy

Studying and Office Supplies

- Backpack or book bag
- Binders
- Book ends
- Bulletin boards for desk and pushpins
- Calculator
- CD/DVD organizers
- Copy paper
- Cord/cable organizers
- Desk lamp and light bulbs
- Desk organizers
- Drawer organizers
- Duct tape
- Glue stick
- Hole punch
- Index cards
- Invisible hanging wire
- Laptop carrying case
- Message board for dorm room door
- Notebooks

- Paper clips
- Pen & pencil holder
- Pencil sharpener
- Pencils, pens
- Picture frames
- Post-it® notes
- Removable mounting tape
- Ruler
- Scissors
- Stackable desk trays
- Stapler
- Storage units
- Tape
- Trash can
- Velcro

Tool Kit

- Duct tape
- Flashlight
- Flat head screwdriver
- Hammer with a claw
- Nails
- Phillip's head screwdriver
- Pliers with wire cutters
- Putty knife
- Screws
- Steel Wool
- Tape measure
- Utility knife with retractable blade

CHAPTER

8

Navigating the Maze

CHECKLIST

❑ Received new student orientation information

❑ Registered for: _____

❑ Responded on: _____

❑ Payment: _____

❑ Booked/reserved hotel or dorm rooms

❑ Arranged for transportion to college

Immediately consult your child and your calendar and then register as soon as possible. There are always some weekends that are more popular than others.

Save More Money by:

- Booking your air travel and hotel rooms well in advance.
- Utilize free dorm room accommodations as much as possible.
- Investigate all the free resources colleges provide such as tutoring, writing courses, career guidance, computers and computer print allowances, concerts, movies, etc.

SOON AFTER YOUR deposit is received to reserve your child's space you will be receiving information about new student orientation. All schools offer a first year student orientation. Some schools offer this during the summer and others offer it between the day you move in and when classes start.

Many colleges and universities are electing to make attendance at a new student orientation mandatory for all incoming first year students. There are optional programs for parents that run concurrently and often there are several different dates for this weekend or two or three-day orientation programs for students and their parents. Even though attending the simultaneous parent program is optional it is highly recommended that you plan on attending.

STUDENT PROGRAM BENEFITS

These programs have been created and designed to help students acclimate to life at college and ensure that they enjoy and benefit from their initial year in college.

Among the benefits are:

- Provide time and an atmosphere that assists students in the challenging transition to college.
- Provide new first year students with a chance to physically get to know the campus, the location of the dorms, classrooms, dining halls, library, etc.
- Help students understand the various programs and resources available.
- Meet other first year students, upperclassmen and other individuals who will mentor them.
- Give students an opportunity to meet with their academic advisors, discuss academic goals and gain advice to help navigate through the academic rigors and challenges.
- Provide an overall understanding of the university and college curriculums, majors, minors and requirements for graduation.
- Create opportunities to be a part of a peer mentor group, meet others and make friends.
- Introduce students to co-curricular activities.
- Help experience a wide variety of on and off campus activities such as store runs, trips into the towns and cities near campuses.
- Create an opportunity to live in a dorm and experience the meal plans.

➤ Sometimes certain college placement tests are taken at these orientations.

➤ Sometimes these sessions include registering for the first semester's classes.

➤ Sometimes this is the time that your child will get their photos taken and have their ID cards created.

PARENT PROGRAMS

While your child is attending the college new student orientation program there are optional Parent Programs offered at the same time.

These programs are designed to:

- Introduce parents to their child's college life
- Give you an opportunity to meet the Deans, professors and other members of the administration
- Have an opportunity to ask questions.

At these orientation sessions your child will often be in lectures, seminars and programs designed for students, while as a parent you will be attending sessions designed for you at the same time. It's important to take notes. You will have so much information given to you that it will be impossible to remember and keep it all straight once you return home.

INVESTIGATE

This is a great time for you to locate, visit and determine . . .

Academic Resources

What are the available resources for helping your child write or research a paper?

What are the tutoring services available—are they free?

- The minute you hear that your child is struggling insist that they contact the instructor to discuss studying strategies.
- Often tutoring services are offered by fellow undergraduate students or peers who have excelled in the subject, for free or at a minimal fee. Quite often past exams and tests can be found in resource centers and used as study tools.

Athletic and Recreation Facilities

Are there any additional costs? Hours?

Banks

Where is the campus branch?

Where are the ATMs?

Bookstores

Where is it located?

Is it the only retail option for book purchases?

Can you pre-order text books to be picked up when school begins?

Is there a used book exchange where books can be re-sold and purchased less expensively?

Campus Map

Pick one up. Determine the location and availability of parking for future visits.

Career Services

Where are the offices?

What services do they provide?

Do they offer workshops for resumé writing or training for interviews?

Do they offer mock interviews?

Do they help place you in internships?

Computers

Does your child need to open up a student account?

Where are the campus computer labs?

Do students get a print allowance and if so, how much and where?

Dining Halls

Where are the dining halls located?

What are their hours?

Which halls are open late for snacks?

Dining Meal Plans

Most universities and colleges want to start students out with the most comprehensive meal plan. In truth, most students don't eat three meals a day for all seven days in the week. A better option is the flexible meal plan that allows your child to have a mix of both dining hall experiences and "dollars" that can be used at other locations.

Most students will have a student ID that can also act as a debit card. You can purchase points, dollars, etc. that will be preloaded onto your child's ID card. In some cases, this money can be used to do laundry, purchase books, computer supplies, snacks and more. Students gain access to their points by using their ID cards like they would a bank debit card.

You can usually arrange to purchase additional dollars as part of your child's account and with the tuition bills. Inquire where you can purchase points or dollars.

Dorms

What are the dimensions and layout of the dorm room?

Do they have single or double beds and can they be bunked?

How big is the closet?

Do they have dressers and how many drawers are in them?

What kind of desk is provided?

How many drawers are in it?

Does the desk have a shelf for books?

Are there sinks in the room?

Is the room carpeted?

Where is the window and do you need drapes?

Where are the bathrooms?

Hotels

Determine the location and names of the nearest hotels.

Laundry Facilities

Where are the laundry facilities?

Are the machines coin fed or do they use the student ID card for payment? How many washers and dryers are there?

Are the machines front loaders? This will make a difference when you purchase laundry detergent.

Medical

Where is Student Health?

Where is the nearest hospital?

Publications

Get a copy of the student independent newspaper. Are there other publications?

Retail Stores

What stores are nearby?

- Nearest drugstore
- Nearest grocery store
- Nearest coffee shop
- Where is the nearest FedEx/Kinko's?

Roommates—Have your child:

Ask your peer group leaders about living with roommates.

Ask for suggestions to ease the transition.

Talk about what to do if your roommate "isn't from heaven."

You may also be invited to get together with other students and their parents in your area who will be students at the same university or college. This is a great time to meet others.

Student Online Accounts

Does your child need to fill out some forms for you to gain access to this account?

Student online accounts contain:

- Academic summaries
- Advisors
- Current class schedule
- External credit and test scores
- Final exam schedule
- Grades
- Transcript information
- Tuition statements
- Financial account summary

When and where will your child's tuition bill appear?

How can you pay?

When do they expect payment to be received and processed by?

Student Safety

Where are the blue lights?

How do you arrange for late night escort service?

Transportation

Where do the campus buses go?

What are the schedules and routes?

What public transportation needs to be considered?

Do you need to consider purchasing a public transportation pass or tokens?

Miscellaneous

Look up in the phone book:

- Taxi cab company
- Balloon delivery service

GOING TO COLLEGE AND MOVING IN

CHAPTER

9

Muscling in on Moving

▼

CHECKLIST

❏ Determine location of your dorm room and where you can park to unload.

❏ Determine the hours and location for picking up your room key.

❏ Determine if your dorm room will have wheeled carts available to help with moving and if there are elevators that will be accessible.

❏ Clearly label and pack cleaning supplies together.

Save More Money by:

● Noting any existing room damage on the room checklist.

● Not losing a dorm key or identity card.

BEFORE YOU'RE ABLE TO UNPACK

BEFORE YOU'LL BE able to unpack your child will need to pick up room keys and important information. They usually are given a room key, mail key and room inspection form and told how to access the building.

The schools usually have students available to help you quickly unload your car and move it to an offsite parking location. There will be hundreds of students moving in and each school has a traffic flow and parking solution that eases the congestion. Plan on moving all the boxes into the dorm, moving your car and then unpacking.

ONCE IN THE ROOM

Inspect the room carefully with your child, making notes of any and all damages or problems. Look for chips, holes, water damage, broken handles, dresser drawers that don't slide, etc. Note this on the form and have your child return the inspection sheet to their dorm representative. If possible request or make a copy of the form. Whatever you don't note as broken, missing, chipped, etc. now may well be considered to be your child's damage when they finally leave the dorm, and it will be charged against the account in May. Unpaid accounts typically prevent registration or graduation.

WARNING

Lost room keys are expensve to replace.

Next

Check the corners of the rooms and closets, if you see little holes, fill them in with steel wool. They could be the doorways for little critters.

I usually use a liquid bleach/cleaner on all the counter tops, the drawers and especially any bathroom surfaces. The rooms are pre-cleaned before you enter—but a second quick cleaning has never hurt anyone.

No matter where we've been the same always holds true—**there is never enough space for everything**—so get creative, get organized, and find a place for everything. Plan on shopping for items that you didn't bring, and plan on taking home some items that there simply is not any room for or an item that the roommate has duplicated.

Create more storage space under the bed

Plan on either racking the bed or lifting it off the floor so as to be able to use the under bed area for storage. Cinder blocks work as well as bed lifters that can be bought commercially either in stores or online. Make sure whatever you do is stable and won't easily fall down.

This is a great location to put some plastic drawer sets. These are sold individually. I find that the drawers that are housed in their own plastic box work the best.

FIND A PLACE FOR EVERYTHING

- Have a bookshelf for books
- Have a binder or shelf for DVDs and CDs
- Have folders and files for loose papers
- Box for receipts
- Plastic boxes to hold snacks
- Plastic quart bags to hold the little things like pencils, markers, sugar packages, etc.

I have each of my girls use a box, plate or some kind of small container to always place their room keys, car keys, glasses and other important items in each time they return to their room. Once a habit, they'll have a harder time misplacing these.

Create some "life files"

An accordion file or binder with pockets works perfect as a "life file." It will help your child keep track of papers that they would normally ignore. Create files or sections for finances, checks, credit card receipts, W-2 and pay stubs, medical, etc.

Room Closet

Create instant shelving with:

- Canvas hanging bags
- Metal shelves
- Cardboard boxes
  - ➤ Neatly cut off the top and gift wrap the outside and inside and place on your upper closet shelf so as the open front is facing you. Now you can not only fill the inside, but also use the top as an additional shelf to place items.
- Plastic boxes
- Fold your bulky sweaters, jeans, etc. and place them on the shelves and not in the drawers.

- Use either cardboard or plastic boxes to store shoes—put flats in one, heels in another and stack the boxes.

  ➤ Don't use shopping bags for storage, they don't stack and they tear.

  ➤ Don't buy super-sized baskets, tubs, or bins—they're too deep and items will always fall to the bottom and get lost.

Desk Area—Create a Workspace

  Make sure it is near an outlet and also internet access

- Have a cup holder for pencils, pens, rulers, etc.
- Put up a bulletin board and a calendar
- Write everything on your calendar
- Paperclip spontaneous notes to your calendar if you don't have time to write them in
- Have your bookshelf nearby
- Put small items like paper clips, tacks, etc. in small boxes
- Use the space under the desk for additional storage for books and supplies

  Always lock your dorm room!

CHAPTER

10

Serious Potpourri

▼

CHECKLIST

❑ Determine method of purchasing text books

❑ Determine your print allowance and where you can utilize it

❑ Determine your college email address

Save More Money by:

- Searching the internet for the best price on the correct edition before purchasing textbooks
- Purchasing used editions of books
- Using the college print allowance

BOOKS AND BOOKSTORE

COLLEGE BOOKSTORES CAN be found in free standing buildings on or near campus or within the student unions/centers. In addition to books, they will also carry a complete selection of apparel, simple supplies and sometimes even dorm supplies and house coffee shops.

It's best to try and purchase your books as early as you can. Remember, everyone will be trying to purchase their text books before classes start, which will mean long lines and long waits. Be prepared to discover that you might not be able to purchase all your books, as some of your books may either be not yet available from the publisher or not enough were ordered by the bookstore for sale.

Students can spend upwards of $900 per semester on books. The university campus bookstores will be the most convenient and the busiest.

Online bookstores often can offer better prices but remember to consider the shipping and handling fees when comparing prices. Purchasing used books can also provide savings.

Campusbooks.com is a good site for your child to check out. It is designed to find the lowest price of the text book that you desire by searching other bookstores and sites.

Make sure that you are purchasing the correct edition of the book, or consult with the professor to determine if another edition will pose a problem before purchasing.

➤ At the end of the semester you can sell your books back for cash. The bookstores, online companies and often college electronic bulletin boards will offer you opportunities to sell your books.

➤ Purchase and use a daily planner for homework assignments and appointments. Make it a habit of carrying it with you everywhere.

COMPUTER CENTER(S)

Most campuses have computer labs scattered in many different locations. They often have extended hours and printers where your child can use their "print allowance."

Whether it is called a computer center or Office of Information Technology there will be a support service that can help your child in case of an emergency. There are people in the computing labs or separate offices who can help with printing, the campus network and connections to the internet, e-mail, telecommunications services, etc.

Too often a lengthy written assignment is lost in a computer crash. Have your child . . .

1. Save their lengthy written paper assignments on their computers
2. Back the assignments up
3. Kate always emails her papers, in their various stages of completion, to herself. If for any reason she can't access them on her computer, she can access them on any other computer through her email. This also allows her to print the papers at any location.

Most students have a paper print allowance and should use it whenever possible.

STUDENT LIFE

College is a wonderful place with many opportunities to meet people and try new things.

There are hundreds of ways your child can get involved in college. There are varsity sports, club teams, artistic clubs, Greek life, music programs, religious organizations, cultural organizations, service groups, international groups, student government and many more.

In addition to the NCAA varsity sports that one can enjoy watching or being a member of, there are numerous opportunities for your child to join a club sport or play intramurals. These vary from organized co-ed soccer to sailing clubs and broom hockey and are an excellent way to meet new friends, exercise and have fun all at the same time.

Lastly, each college and university will also be host to hundreds of events each year such as sports, movies, comedy, drama, music events, debates and lectures. Quite often there are also exhibits of artifacts and art for everyone to enjoy.

TIP

Join university clubs, the pre-law or pre-med club, the business or marketing club, etc. The friends that you will make and networking are invaluable.

Beth joined Boston University's Minorities in Hospitality organization and as a member was able to travel with other members to Seattle for the annual conference. She was a freshman and even though she was not planning to seek a job while at the conference, she decided to meet with recruiters and go through the interview process. The recruiters were delighted to meet someone in their first year of college. They offered advice and tips on future internships and what successful job applicants should accomplish during their 4 years in college. This trip really helped Beth focus and helped her secure those "prized" internships.

CHAPTER

11

Checking
for the
Safety Net

▼

CHECKLIST

- ❑ Discuss Stress
- ❑ Discuss Health Safety
- ❑ Discuss Door Room Safety
- ❑ Discuss Personal Safety
- ❑ Discuss Risk of Assault
- ❑ Discuss Identity Safety
- ❑ Discuss Car Safety
- ❑ Discuss Bike Safety
- ❑ Discuss Extreme Weather

ALONG WITH FINANCES, safety is an important talk every parent needs to have with a child going off to college for the first time. Until now the security of home, parental experience and familiar surroundings have given your child a sense of safety. College will change all of this. Your child will be expected to share space with a stranger in new surroundings and might be an unsuspecting victim to preying thieves. College students need to use common sense, be alert and use caution. They will be at risk for bodily harm from accidents, sickness and potential assaults, with the possibility of having wallets, property and even identities stolen. They could be involved in car, bike and pedestrian accidents as well as exposed to unaccustomed and severe weather. Students must be educated and made aware of these risks.

STRESS

Every child is going to experience stress from trying to do everything or too much in a short period of time, and it will inevitably come around midterms. This is the perfect time for a box to be received with goodies from home.

A student should also:

- Take breaks and change the environment by going for a walk, eating a meal or doing some other activity for relaxation.
- Relax or exercise.
- Keep to a routine, eat meals at the same time.
- Get good night's sleep.
- Think positively and smile.
- Break school assignments down into manageable portions and tackle one portion or problem at a time.
- Join study groups and talk about problems. Often one learns better when trying to explain something to others.
- Plan ahead and, if needed, meet with a tutor.

Students should stick to a routine, eating nutritious meals and get a good night's sleep.

HEALTH SAFETY

Unfortunately, the reality is that our students will spend little time cleaning and washing clothing. In fact, for some the only time the bed might be made is when the child first moves in and then again at Thanksgiving.

It's also a fact that viruses and germs can stick around for several weeks.

Combine both of these with stress and you have the perfect conditions for coming down with the flu or a cold.

Wiping down a cell phone and hand held iPod won't prevent sickness, but it might help minimize it. Laundry, when done on a regular basis, will help reduce germs.

It is recommended that:

➤ Undergarments should be washed in hot water.

➤ Sheets and bedding should be washed at least once a week. If the student doesn't make the bed and dirty feet and shoes are landing on the sheets, washing bedding is even more important.

➤ Students shouldn't share cups, water bottles or food.

➤ Students should be mindful of food
spoilage and never eat anything that
has mold on it.

DORM ROOM SAFETY

- Always lock windows when you leave.
- Always lock your dorm room, even to go to the restroom.
- Always keep your cell phone charged in case of emergency.
- Take a photo of your dorm room once you've settled in. This will make it easier to remember if something is stolen.

FIRE SAFETY

Avoid Accidentally Starting a Fire

- Make sure that you use UL-listed surge strips.
- Don't overload extension cords and power outlets.
- Don't burn candles.
- Keep clothing and items away from heaters and hot surfaces.
- Be aware that laptops have started fires.
- Do not leave electrical appliances like irons or curling irons on and unattended.
- Don't let curtains or clothing cover lampshades or light bulbs.

In Case of a Fire

- Never ignore a fire alarm.
- Note the location of the nearest stairwell, fire extinguisher and fire alarm.
- Before opening the door always feel the knob first. A hot knob indicates a close fire and the need to keep the door closed. If your door is too hot to open, put wet towels around the doorframe to keep the smoke out and try to escape through a window or get someone's attention.
- If smoke is present, keep low and try to crawl out.
- Do not use elevators during a fire, use the stairs.
- Do not go back in a room on fire.

PERSONAL SAFETY

Reducing Risk of Assault:

- According to the Rape, Abuse, and Incest National Network (RAINN), "1 in 6 women and 1 in 33 men will be sexually assaulted in a lifetime and college women are 4 times more likely to be sexually assaulted."

RAINN www.rainn.org 202-544-3064 suggests students:

- Know your surroundings and avoid secluded areas.
- Avoid walking or being in isolated areas by yourself.

- Make sure your cell phone is on you and works.
- Try walking with an air of confidence.
- Don't make yourself vulnerable by loading yourself with more than you can carry.
- Note location of blue lights on campus.
- When going to a party, go with a group of friends, arrive together, check in and leave together.
- Never drink from any open bottle, cup or can.
- Always open the drink container yourself and keep it with you. If you put it down, get another new can.

Additional RAINN 2008 Spring Break Tip's for Students

Get to know your surroundings before you go out and learn a well-lit route back to your hotel or rental property.

1. Always carry emergency cash and keep phone numbers for local cab companies handy. Form a buddy system with close friends and agree on a secret "butt in" signal for uncomfortable situations.
2. Trust your instincts. If you feel unsafe in any situation, go with your gut.
3. Avoid being alone or isolated with someone you don't know or trust.
4. Don't accept drinks from people you don't know or trust.
5. Never leave your drink unattended, and if you do lose sight of it, get a new one.

6. Always watch your drink being prepared.
7. Try to buy drinks in bottles, which are harder to tamper with than cups or glasses.
8. Avoid using music headphones in both ears so that you can be more aware of your surroundings, especially if you are walking alone.

Date Rape

Date Rape is a felony and occurs when one person forces another person to have sex. In many cases of date rape, the victim knows the attacker, chooses to spend time with him and sometimes even goes out more than once with the attacker. The confusion is that once a victim tries to stop the sexual act or say "no" the sexual act becomes rape and is considered a criminal offense. Men in particular need to understand this and cease the sexual act before it becomes a criminal offense.

Alcohol is often involved in date rapes. Drinking can loosen inhibitions, dull common senses and for some people allow aggressive tendencies to surface.

Drugs also play a part. Sometimes they can be mixed into drinks to make a person black out and forget things that happen. Both girls and guys who have been given these drugs report feelings paralyzed, having blurred vision and lack of memory.

Remember:

- Never drink from an open punch bowl.
- Go out with a group of friends.
- Don't break the law and drink under the age of 21. Stay sober and aware of your surroundings.

- Take a self-defense course.
- www.rad-systems.com offers comprehensive women-only courses that begins with awareness, prevention, and risk reduction and risk avoidance, while progressing on to the basics of hands-on defense training. The average cost for the basic physical defense program for women is about $25.00. Some communities offer the program through their local police department. Colleges and universities sometimes offer the class as a credit course. See the web site for more program locations and more details.

IDENTITY SAFETY

Identity theft is the fastest growing crime in the US.

The US Department of Justice web site provides several pages dedicated to details of identity theft and identity fraud.

They say "to reduce or minimize the risk of becoming a victim remember 4 steps and the word SCAM."

S   Be stingy about giving out your personal information to others unless you have a reason to trust them.

C   Check your personal financial information regularly.

A   Ask periodically for a copy of your credit report.

M   Maintain careful records of your banking and financial accounts.

Source the US Department of Justice website
www.usdoj.gov/criminal/fraud

In addition:

- Never leave a credit card receipt at an establishment or in a shopping bag.
- Don't leave mail in your mailbox to be picked up by your mail carrier. Instead personally drop it into a mailbox. All too often thieves take outgoing mail, looking for check payments to obtain account numbers, signature and other valuable information. Often a remittance slip may also contain the credit card number.
- Check your credit reports at least once every 4 months. There are 3 credit bureaus that each give an individual the right to obtain the report for free.
- Never give out credit card information or personal information to unsolicited callers or emails. Rarely do companies need additional information from established account holders.
- Always shred pre-approved credit card offers.
- Don't give retailers your phone number and address when asked.
- Always check *no* for "can we share this information with others" on the web and retail sites when making purchases.
- Reduce the amount of information that is shared between companies by selecting the *no* option.

- Photo copy the front and backs of every credit card, driver's license and insurance card in your billfold. If your wallet is stolen, the customer service phone numbers are often located on the back of the credit cards. Make sure you can read these numbers. Keep one copy with you at school and another home with you parent or in another safe location at another site.
- Make sure ATM cards don't access all accounts.
- Create an excel chart listing every expected statement and bill and when they are to be received, checking off the bills and statements as they arrive. Plan on calling the card company or bank if one doesn't appear. It's common for thieves to change billing addresses to allow themselves an opportunity to not only keep you from seeing the fraudulent charges but to also have these purchases shipped to the new billing address.

If your wallet or purse is stolen:

- If your identity and/or credit cards have been stolen, immediately call the three credit card reporting agencies and alert them. Ask for the fraud alert to be put onto your account. Call each credit card company, DMV, etc.
- Scrutinize each and every credit card and bill statement that you receive.
- File a police report.

- Send a registered letter letter of release acknowledging the stolen card and fraudulent charges and stating that you will not be held responsible for them.
- For any new cards, make sure you get new account numbers and new passwords.
- If bank checks are stolen, stop payment on them, but beware of the routing numbers and other information found on the checks. A safer solution is to inform the bank, provide them with a list of checks that you wrote and want to clear and cancel the account. Open a new account with new information and new checks.

I had an individual take a payroll check written to his daughter, make new checks using my bank information with his address and cashed them in Washington, DC. Since the checks were being sent through the mail no picture ID was necessary and I didn't know of the cashed checks until I received my bank statement. Fortunately it was a corporate account and the bank moved swiftly to catch the individuals and recover all the money.

Insurance cards should be considered as valuable as a credit card and any loss needs to be reported immediately. There are horror stories of thieves impersonating others and using their health care benefits. Monitor and look over your health insurance statements verifying their accuracy.

Your personal organizer, Blackberry, cell phone

- Make a back up file of everything on your computer. Update once a week.
- If you carry a paper organizer, clean it out; removing receipts, deposit slips etc. and file everything into its proper place once a week.
- Use a password for access to your cell phone.
- Consider insurance. All four of us have Blackberries and the insurance for them. Ann's phone screen went blank, and we were thankful for the insurance that allowed for a new replacement at no additional charge. The phone company was able to retrieve and transfer all the data to the new phone.
- If you think you have lost your phone or it has been stolen, immediately call your service provider, they can disable the phone immediately. A couple of years ago I thought I had lost my cell phone in the airport. I called, disabled my number and went on my trip. Upon returning to my car in the airport lot, I found my phone was able to re-enable it with a simple phone call.
- If you do lose your phone, send a mass email to everyone to inform family and friends that you have a new phone number.
- File a police report in case it is necessary to dispute a future bill.

Lost keys

- Never label keys or have an identification tag hanging with them.
- Leave a spare house and car key with your family.
- Never attach the store keychain membership cards to your house or car keys. If you lose your keys these membership cards could give the thief your personal information as well.
- Disable the alarm that sounds when you lock your car. If you lose your car keys in a parking lot, it will be easier for the thief to locate your car by its alarm.

COMPUTER, SOFTWARE AND INTERNET SAFETY

- Never give your social security number to any site that requests it. If that information is needed, go to the company's web site to investigate for contact information.
- Never give email username or email passwords to anyone.
- Change your password regularly. Use combinations of symbols, numbers and lower and upper case letters.
- If you use Windows operating system, make sure your Windows version is the most current.
- Phishing is typically carried out by email or instant messaging and is an attempt to acquire personal information such as social security numbers, usernames, and passwords,

credit card numbers, etc by pretending to be a legitimate, recognizable company.

- Be especially suspicious for deletions or additions in web site names that are soliciting this info such as "AOL live" versus "AOL." Also be wary of mis-spelled words or poor use of grammar.
- Be aware of people behind you while withdrawing money from ATM machines, cashing checks or using credit cards. A true thief will be pretending to talk on his cell phone while he is taking photos of your card and check numbers. Use discretion when handing these items over to clerks and be aware of the activities of persons close to you.

BIKE SAFETY AND POTENTIAL PROBLEMS

- Register your bike with the make, model and serial number with campus police.
- Always wear shoes when biking. Never go barefoot or wear flip-flops when biking.
- Be careful that your pant legs or skirt can't get tangled in the bike's chain or wheel's spokes.
- Lock your bike with a good heavy-duty bike lock in a visible location. Lock it through the wheel and frame. Recently, I passed a bike frame locked to a pole. Note I said frame; the wheels, seat and handlebars were missing. This is an extreme example but an expensive bike needs to secure before leaving it. Lock the bike through the wheel and frame. If you lock only the wheel, the bike may be stolen

and you'll be left with a wheel. If you lock only the frame you could come back to find a wheel missing. Use as well lit an area as possible.

- When away for weekends or breaks, move your bike to a more secure area—perhaps inside your dorm room or apartment.
- Never talk on your cell phone while riding the bike.
- Pedestrians always have the right of way.
- Always ride your bike with traffic.
- Always obey the traffic signals and stop signs.
- Wear a helmet.
- If riding a bike in the evening make sure it has a light in the front and back so you are visible to cars.
- Be extremely careful when riding past driveways and parking lots. Cars pulling or backing out might not see you.

CAR SAFETY AND POTENTIAL PROBLEMS

Car Accidents

If you are in an accident, never leave the scene without first calling the police. If you feel compromised, stay in your car until the police come. Exchange information with the other driver and take photos of the damage and the other car's license plate. Your cell phone sometimes can act as a camera; if your cell phone does not have a camera function, keep a small disposable camera in your glove compartment. Plan on calling your insurance and the other person's insurance if mandated.

Additional Car Issues

Does your child know what to do if he or she gets a parking ticket? It's worth understanding that parking tickets can't be ignored. There is a short amount of time when one is allowed to either pay or contest it. Ignored tickets quickly increase in price and are treated as unpaid bills sent to collection agencies. At some time in the future, whether re-registering the car or renewing a license, the new higher unpaid ticket will find you.

What do you do if the car is towed away? Do you have a credit card or cash to pay for the ticket, tow charge, etc. Look for a sign identifying the towing company or a number to call if towed. If you were not parked illegally or in a place where a violation could lead to towing, call the police.

WEATHER DISASTERS

I never really paid attention to weather as a safety threat until Hurricane Ike went straight through Texas A & M in College Station, Texas where Ann is living. Ann quickly learned how to prepare for a hurricane and this material is now part of this chapter. The University cancelled classes; everyone was sent home if commuting or to a dorm room with instructions.

Each storm has different circumstances dictating what to before, during and after it occurs.

Complete information can be found at the Federal Emergency Management Agency (also known as FEMA www. Fema.gov).

*Note: a weather **watch** is a notification that a weather pattern is possible. One needs to remain alert, stayed tuned to advisories and may have time to shop and make preparations. A **warning** indicates that the specified weather has been sighted or indicated by weather radar, and shelter should be sought immediately.*

FEMA INSTRUCTIONS:

Hurricane
With adequate time, shop and be prepared with:
- Bottled water
- Food that can be eaten without heat or refrigeration
- Manual can opener
- Flashlight
- Batteries
- Charged cell phone—although if cell towers are down you'll have poor calling ability
- Extra clothes
- First aid kit
- Money
- Gas in your car

Hurricane Warning is Issued:
- Close curtains to prevent flying glass.
- Secure windows and doors.
- Close all interior doors and brace external doors.
- Fill your bathtub with water and other large containers with water that can be used for cleaning or flushing toilets if necessary.

Tornadoes

Most tornadoes strike quickly, with little or no warning.

- Go to a pre-designated shelter such as a basement, or the lowest section of a building. If there is no basement go to the center of an interior room and try and put as many walls between you and the outside.
- Seek shelter under a table of desk to protect yourself from flying or falling debris.
- If you are in vehicle get out immediately and go to the lowest floor of a nearby building.
- If you are outside with no shelter, lie flat in a nearby ditch or depression and cover your head with your hands.
- Keep away from overhead lights and electoral cords.

Earthquakes

Most earthquakes strike suddenly, and also without warning.

Most related injuries and deaths are the result of collapsing walls, flying glass and other falling objects.

- If in a moving vehicle, avoid stopping near buildings, overhead wires, streetlamps, etc. Try and stop in an open area and stay in the vehicle.
- If indoors, drop to the floor, take cover by getting under a sturdy table or other piece of furniture and hold on until the shaking stops.

- Stay away from glass, overhead lights and electrical cords.
- Do not use elevators.
- If outdoors, stay there and move away from buildings, wires, lights, etc.

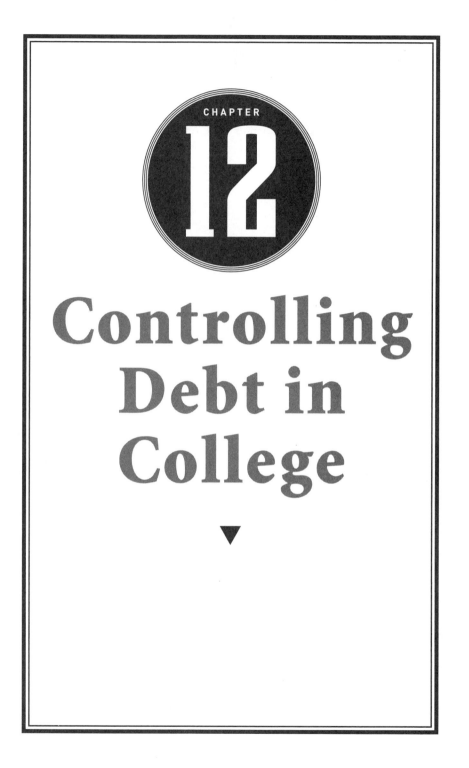

CHAPTER

12

Controlling
Debt in
College

▼

CHECKLIST

❑ Determine weekly cash expenditures

❑ Determine the location of the grocery store with the lowest prices and best sales

❑ Get organized

Save More Money by:

- Shopping frugally—see page 152
- Watching how you eat out—see page 154
- Using coupons

MOST STUDENTS NOW graduate from college with more than a fantastic education and a piece of parchment paper. They are graduating in debt, owing thousands of dollars in student loans and high interest credit card debt. Chapter 5 discusses finances, student budgeting and the importance of discussing money management with the college bound child. This chapter will offer tips on how to stretch those precious dollars and spend fewer of them.

SPENDING LESS

These are tough times and as parents we want the best for our children. We want them graduating with a fantastic education and a sense of security that comes from growing into responsible adults who can manage and live within their means.

Students must sit down, do money management and learn to live within their means. Spending within a budget will require planning and will power. A conscious decision must be made with each and every purchase, determining if the item to be procured is a necessity or just desired.

How much money is spent each week?

Does the student know how much is spent each and every day? Probably not. It's the rare college student who sits down and plans daily expenditures.

It's imperative that students understand how much they spend each week.

The easiest way to determine this is to monitor and spend an allocated amount of cash for one week. Have your child put a weekly allowance (in cash) into an envelope. Give the credit cards a vacation by putting them away and, for one week, only use the cash in the envelope for all expenditures. Put all receipts from these expenditures into the envelope holding the money. If the cash has been spent before the weekend, your student needs to sit down and analyze the purchases. Perhaps morning coffee or tea at $4.00 a cup or pizza once a week might need to be eliminated or minimized.

Unless another source of income can be identified, the student must learn to spend less. Keep trying this exercise until at day 7 there is still money left in the envelope.

> Tuck a $20.00 bill somewhere in your wallet as emergency money.

> This won't be easy but you will purchase less impulsively when using cash.

CHART OF EXPENDITURES

Day	Amount Spent	Items cash spent on	Necessity	Desire
Monday				
Tuesday				
Wednesday				
Thursday				
Friday				
Saturday				
Sunday				
Total of allowance				
Total spent				
Difference				

SHOPPING

Money can be saved by

- Watching for retail store sales especially the tax free "holidays".
- Shopping on-line. Look for free delivery and free shipping on returns.
- Buy demos and display models with warranties.
- Look for used or reconditioned items with warranties.
- Purchase energy efficient light bulbs that will save money by lasting longer.
- Participate in refund offers. Keep the original sales receipt, note the expiration date of the offer and determine if you need a "proof of purchase" from the packaging.

Comparison shop before making any large purchases.

Textbooks are expensive

Save money by:

- Shopping online remembering to consider shipping and handling charges when comparing prices.
- Use campusbooks.com to find the lowest price for a textbook.
- Purchase used editions of books.
- Some international editions are less expensive.
- Free textbooks online might be available for a course. These books allow students the

ability to download and print any part of the textbook.

- Some textbooks are available as print on demand at a reasonable cost.
- Some textbooks are packaged with workbooks and CD. Check with the professor to deem the necessity of the additional items. Perhaps you can purchase just the used textbook without the CD or workbook. Perhaps you can purchase the components separately.

The following sites offer savings on textbooks:

- www.Campusbookswap.org
- www.BooksOnCampus.com (partnered with Facebook)
- www.Ecampus.com
- www.cheapestbooks.com
- www.half.ebay.com
- www.buyusedbooks.com

You're on a meal plan

If you are on a meal plan—the obvious way to save money is to use the meal plan to your advantage. Plan to eat your meals in the dining hall and take food with you for your snack needs. Many plans offer guest meals that should be used. If you need a late night snack, grab a piece of fruit or additional sweet to take with you to the dorm. Most meal plans have dollars that can be spent at accepted eateries and restaurant on campus. Monitor spending these "dollars" and avoid the more expensive convenience stores affiliated with the plan.

Spending less when eating out

When with a group, always ask for a separate check. Usually a bill is split by the number of participants and rarely will represent the actual amount ordered by individuals.

- Consider ordering appetizers.
- Considering splitting an entrée with another person. Restaurant portions are often large and one meal could be perfect for two people to share.
- Take home a doggie bag with your left-overs.
- Consider eating when a dinner or lunch special is available.
- Whenever a situation is appropriate, take left over pre-packaged salt, pepper, condiments, crackers, paper napkins, straws, wet wipes for use in the dorm room.

Don't purchase
- Anything from vending machines.
- Bottled water. Rather buy a water filter and refill a BPT free container.
- Paper towels, use a dishtowel or paper napkins that you obtain for free from dining hall, fast food restaurants, etc.

You have a kitchen as part of your living arrangement and are not on a meal plan
When purchasing food:
- Buy bulk paper and food items that you will be able to use or consume during the semester.

- Plan your meals and prepare a shopping list, don't impulse buy.
- Don't shop on an empty stomach when everything will be tempting.
- Stick to the outside aisles of the grocery store where the essentials are kept. Note that you will have to travel through lots of tempting items to reach the milk aisle.
- Purchase raw, whole foods and cook a meal from scratch. Usually food that is pre-prepared and ready to eat or frozen, is costly.
- Consider buying day old bread. The new bread that you would otherwise buy will be a day old tomorrow.
- Grocery stores often lower the sale price of meat in the afternoon if the item will be passing "its sell by" date. The meat is still good and in fact a few hours earlier would have sold for full price.
- Clip and use coupons. Sign up for your store's savings club. Find out when your store's weekly sales circular will come out. Look at it online, plan meals around the specials and shop the store weekly specials.
- Don't purchase pre-cut or prepared meats or vegetable packages.
- Cook and eat vegetarian meals at least once a week.
- Always comparison shop for the best value.
- Purchase multipacks of gum and mints rather than the single packs.
- If getting together for a meal suggests that everyone contribute and share something.

A word about coupons.

I'm a coupon clipper and save additional money each week by using coupons found in the Sunday paper insert, our local store's web site, manufacturer's web sites and at various coupon websites. Real savings can be realized when you combine a coupon and store special or "double coupon value". Sometimes, when a rebate is included, I'm getting the product for free.

> ➤ Note that not all stores will accept Internet coupons.

> ➤ Even with coupons sometimes manufacturer brands still have a higher selling price than store brands.

I rarely buy dishwashing detergent, laundry soap, Kleenex or toilet paper at full price. I wait for the drugstores to have their weekly special. This past week our 16 oz. dishwashing soap was advertized as "buy 1 at $1.79 get 1 free. Add to it a coupon for 30 cents and I was purchasing 2 for 1.49 a savings of $2.09. At the same CVS/pharmacy, Kleenex was on sale for 89 cents each. Once again I had a coupon for $1.00 off the purchase of 5. The total cost was $3.45 or 69 cents a box or a savings of $3.95.

> Only purchase an item if you need it and not because it is on sale or cheap.

TRAVEL

Cars

Cars are expensive and the easiest way to save money is to leave the car home. If that is not an option here are some additional tips to save money:

Getting better gas mileage:
- Driving the speed limit
- Making sure car tires are properly inflated
- Removing excess items and weight from a car
- Using the recommended motor oil
- Maintaining the car; replacing air filters, spark plugs, etc as suggested by the car manufacturer

Spending less on gas:
- Purchasing the recommended octane level gasoline.
- Find the cheapest gas near you on the web and remember you can often find less expensive gas if you visit gas stations that are "not convenient", but rather further away from a highway exit, don't have a service bay or are further out of town.
- Discount stores, warehouse stores and grocery stores often have gas pumps affiliated with them. These offer a cheaper option and sometimes the more you spend in the grocery store, the more of a discount you'll receive per gallon at the pump.
- Take advantage of gas station customer days that offer usually a 5-cent or more per gallon

savings on gas purchased on a specific day of the week.

- Pay cash and take advantage of gas stations that offer better pricing for cash transactions.

The government web site www.fueleconomy.gov spells out in detail exact savings per gallon. Two examples from their web site are: "You can assume that each 5 mph you drive over 60 mph is like paying an additional 26 cents per gallon of gas" and "If you keep your tires inflated you can save up to $0.11 per gallon."

You can use less gas if you:

- Plan on walking short distance rather than driving.
- Park the car and don't use drive through options that will leave a car idling while waiting for your turn.
- Avoid using air conditioning while driving in town.
- Consolidate errands and combine trips.
- Commute using mass transport.

If traveling by car

Service the car before the long trip home to prevent paying higher prices at a gas station on your trip

- Check fuses
- Check fluid levels
- Inflate tires to their proper pressure
- Fill tank with gas
- Check the windshield wiper fluid

- Take snacks and beverages with you
- Consider offering another student a ride with you and split the cost of gas and tolls

Planes

Saving money on tickets:
- Sign up for airline programs and start saving miles and points.
- Sign up for email special promotions and book your flights during these advertized specials—usually once month.
- Book ahead for busy holidays and spring break and be prepared to volunteer your seat in exchange of a later flight and free roundtrip ticket.
- Comparison shop for the best ticket price. Look at travel sites such as Expedia, Travelocity and Orbitz. Check individual airline sites that often offer better deals than any of the above. If you can be flexible, trips with multiple stops will be a less expensive alternative to non-stop flights.
- Booking online with Travelocity, Orbitz, and others will incur a booking fee.
- Buying a ticket over the phone will cost more even if you don't get a paper ticket.
- Check aggregator sites or sites that run searches on numerous other sites simultaneously such as:
  - ➤ **www.kayak.com** which searches over 100 travel sites
  - ➤ **www.bookingbuddy.com** which looks at 29 aggregators
  - ➤ **www.independenttraveler.com**

- Mail yourself the ticket information and make sure you have a seat assignment. Not being able to select a seat could indicate an oversold position and another opportunity to "volunteer your seat."
- Avoid seat assignment charges by selecting your final seat at online check-in.
- Consider giving up your seat and traveling later in the day.

> On my business trips I often book the first flight Monday morning and I've learned to automatically go to the gate agent and offer up my seat should they have a need. Once in LA the agent responded immediately (2 hours prior to the flight) that they needed my seat, gave me my voucher good for a free round trip anywhere in the US and had a driver transport three others and myself to a different airport to catch a flight. I arrived back home one hour later than my originally scheduled flight.

> Consider traveling with carry on luggage if traveling by plane.

A word about luggage

Most airlines restrict carry ons to one bag and an additional smaller personal piece in addition to size

and weight restrictions. Food Bags containing purchased food are not considered in this count.

- REI, Hudson Trail Outfitters and the
  Container Store all offer what is called a
  "multi-part bag". When fully assembled
  this bag can easily be rolled thought the
  airport and security as a single unit. Their
  advantage is that you can unzip portions or
  parts that can become additional duffel bags,
  day bags etc. High Sierra and Eagle Creek
  manufacturer several versions of these bags.
- Checking luggage. Fees for checking a first
  and second bag make traveling with carry
  on more attractive. See each airlines websites
  to determine the fees for checking first and
  second bags.
- Compare the cost of checking luggage versus
  shipping luggage. FedEx, UPS and others now
  ship luggage at competitive rates.

> ➤ Take some food with you on the plane.
>   Few airlines are serving anything other
>   than beverages for free. When bringing
>   food through TSA screening, remember
>   you can't bring in bottle of fluids and
>   salad dressing packages need to be
>   placed in your bag of fluids.

> ➤ Remember your headphones and
>   blankets; airlines are also beginning to
>   charge for these.

Hotels
Saving money at hotels:
- Don't use the hotel phone or internet and have the hotel remove the automatic charges for telephone and internet.
- Have the hotel remove the resort fee if you won't be using the golf course or tennis courts.
- Have the hotel remove the gratuities charge from the bill and leave tips for maid service in your room.
- Don't use the minibar. Many hotels now use an automated minibar that will automatically assess a charge to your room any time an item is lifted off of its resting pace in the cabinet.
- Check the minibar when you arrive to determine that you won't be charged for items that you did not use.
- Don't use room service. Room service meals incur a delivery charge in addition to a 18% gratuity charge and sales tax.
- Look at the bill when it is slipped under your hotel door and ask for an explanation of any charges you don't understand.
- Immediately sign up for hotel loyalty programs.

CHAPTER

13

Changing the Tire in the 21st Century

▼

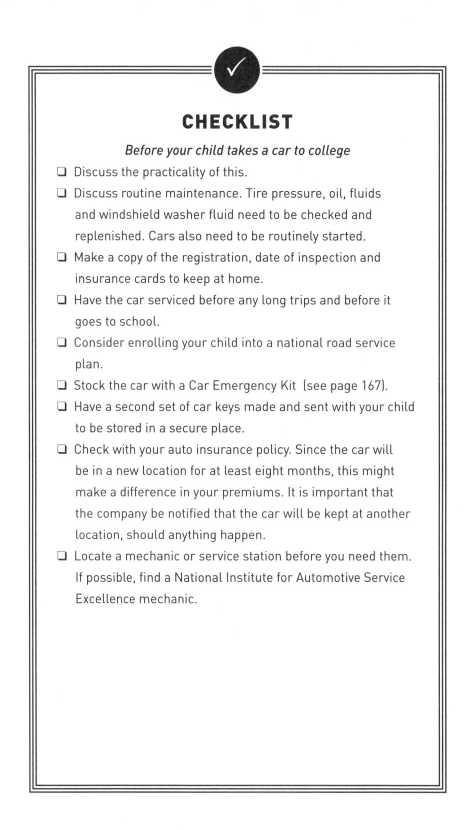

CHECKLIST

Before your child takes a car to college

❏ Discuss the practicality of this.

❏ Discuss routine maintenance. Tire pressure, oil, fluids and windshield washer fluid need to be checked and replenished. Cars also need to be routinely started.

❏ Make a copy of the registration, date of inspection and insurance cards to keep at home.

❏ Have the car serviced before any long trips and before it goes to school.

❏ Consider enrolling your child into a national road service plan.

❏ Stock the car with a Car Emergency Kit (see page 167).

❏ Have a second set of car keys made and sent with your child to be stored in a secure place.

❏ Check with your auto insurance policy. Since the car will be in a new location for at least eight months, this might make a difference in your premiums. It is important that the company be notified that the car will be kept at another location, should anything happen.

❏ Locate a mechanic or service station before you need them. If possible, find a National Institute for Automotive Service Excellence mechanic.

> A car will be a distraction. It will be
  expensive and it may take away from
  the college experience, especially in the
  early years.

> Some college and universities restrict
  or prohibit freshman from bringing cars
  with them their first year.

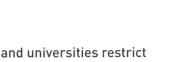

PARKING

MOST UNIVERSITIES AND colleges have an Office
of Parking that is responsible for all parking
lots, garages and marked spaces on campus. Your
child will need to register the car with this office and
purchase a parking pass. Usually passes are designated for specific lots.

In certain states, such as Massachusetts, the state
law requires every non-resident student who operates

a motor vehicle registered in another state to fill out and file a form with the local police station.

There is usually no fee for this registration, but failure to comply can be punished with a fine. Your child can determine if the state the college is in requires additional forms to be filed.

➤ When a vehicle is parked on a university property, there may be motorist assistance. This assistance could be in the form of jump starting your car, helping to unlock it or helping to arrange for a tow. Have your child determine if this assistance is available and if there are fees for it.

➤ Remember the busiest days of travel (and therefore the most treacherous) are:

- The Wednesday before Thanksgiving
- The Sunday after Thanksgiving
- The Friday before Memorial Day
- The Tuesday before Labor Day

Before you lend your car to a friend; verify that your car insurance will cover any potential problem or accident that might happen when you're not the driver.

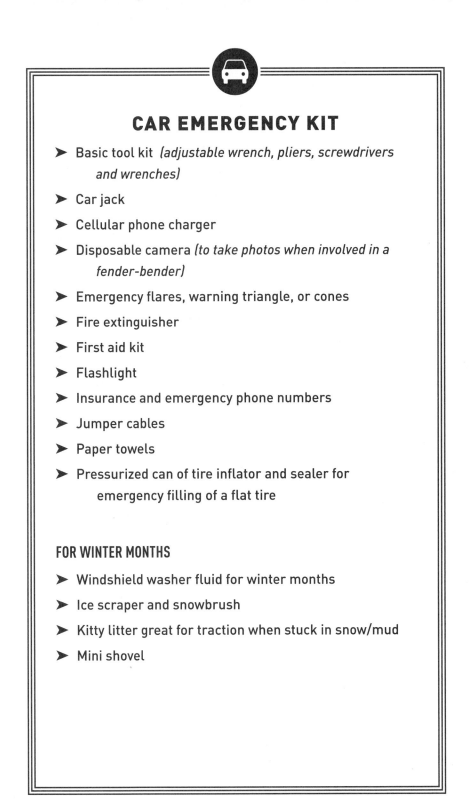

CAR EMERGENCY KIT

➤ Basic tool kit *(adjustable wrench, pliers, screwdrivers and wrenches)*

➤ Car jack

➤ Cellular phone charger

➤ Disposable camera *(to take photos when involved in a fender-bender)*

➤ Emergency flares, warning triangle, or cones

➤ Fire extinguisher

➤ First aid kit

➤ Flashlight

➤ Insurance and emergency phone numbers

➤ Jumper cables

➤ Paper towels

➤ Pressurized can of tire inflator and sealer for emergency filling of a flat tire

FOR WINTER MONTHS

➤ Windshield washer fluid for winter months

➤ Ice scraper and snowbrush

➤ Kitty litter great for traction when stuck in snow/mud

➤ Mini shovel

ROAD TRIP

Before your child decides to take a road trip

Make sure to . . .

- Tell someone their itinerary, especially departure dates and times and expected dates and times of return.
- Have the car serviced and checked—especially tire pressure, engine fluids and windshield wiper fluids.
- Check fuses.
- Fill gas tank.
- Take a car phone and phone charger.
- Have map and know an alternate route should it be needed. Ann writes the driving instructions on index cards that are easier to read while driving than a map.
- Check fuses.
- Have change and single dollar bills readily available for any potential tolls.
- Use common sense and safety.
- Take snacks and beverages with you.

Getting better gas mileage:

- Driving the speed limit.
- Making sure car tires are properly inflated.
- Removing excess items and weight from a car
- Using the recommended motor oil.
- Maintaining the car; replacing air filters, spark plugs, etc as suggested by the car manufacturer.
- Accelerate slowly.

INFORMATION YOU NEED TO TELL YOUR CHILD

CHAPTER

14

Travel

Don't Just Get Carried Away

▼

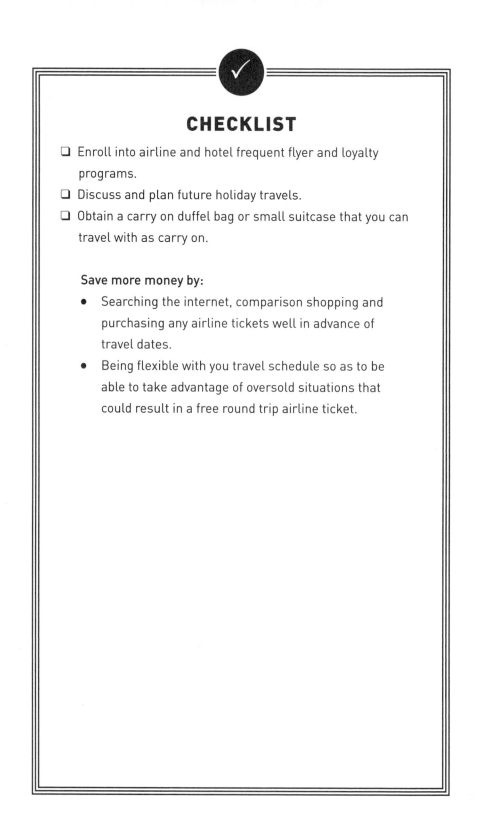

CHECKLIST

- ❑ Enroll into airline and hotel frequent flyer and loyalty programs.
- ❑ Discuss and plan future holiday travels.
- ❑ Obtain a carry on duffel bag or small suitcase that you can travel with as carry on.

Save more money by:

- Searching the internet, comparison shopping and purchasing any airline tickets well in advance of travel dates.
- Being flexible with you travel schedule so as to be able to take advantage of oversold situations that could result in a free round trip airline ticket.

TRAVEL

THERE WILL BE many different ways students travel between home and school. These range from being driven by mom and dad or catching a ride with a friend to riding a bus, train or airplane. Plan ahead with your child. Understand what the various pricing and timing options are with today's security concerns and weather issues. Sometimes a bus or train may be a very viable option. If so, know where the local bus and train stations are. Most importantly, have a communications plan. You will be surprised at what can be accomplished with planning and communications.

> Make sure your child tells you his or her travel plans. Most students purchase tickets online. It's a good idea to have them automatically have the carrier send you an email confirmation when purchasing tickets.

> Within your email system create an email folder titled travel and move travel confirmations to this folder. It's easy to find no matter where you are or if your child lost the information. Have your child create the same. This information can be accessed from any computer.

> Sign your child up now for frequent flyer programs.

AIRLINES

Airlines		Frequent Flyer #	Pin #
Air Canada	www.aircanada.com 1-888-247-2262		
AirTran	www.airtran.com 1-800-247-8726		
American Airlines	www.aa.com 1-800-433-7300		
American Trans Air	www.ata.com 1-800-225-2995		
British Airways	www.britishairways.com 1-800-247-9297		
Continental Airlines	www.continental.com 1-800-525-0280		
Delta Air Lines	www.delta.com 1-800-221-1212		

Airlines		Frequent Flyer #	Pin #
JetBlue Airways	www.jetblue.com 1-800-538-2583		
Northwest Airlines	www.nwa.com 1-800-225-2525		
Southwest Airlines	www.southwest.com 1-800-435-9792		
Ted Airlines	www.flyted.com 1-800-225-5833		
United Airlines	www.united.com 1-800-241-6522		
USAir	www.usairways.com 1-800-428-4322		

TRAINS

Trains		Guest Rewards #	Pin #
Amtrak	www.amtrak.com 1-800-523-8720		

Arrange ahead of time for cabs when leaving for holidays and semester breaks. Remember everyone will be trying to hail cabs on the street.

TRAVEL TIPS

Before you leave for a trip make sure you have . . .
- Photo ID
- Tickets with you
- Keys

- Unplug all electrical equipment except your refrigerator.
- Empty your refrigerator of any food that can spoil.
- Give your family or a friend a copy of your itinerary, *ESPECIALLY* your departure and expected arrival times.
- Take out the trash.
- Have cash available.
- Take your phone, phone charger, glasses, contacts and medications with you as a carry on rather than packing.
- REMEMBER AIRLINES AND HOTELS **OVERBOOK**.
- Get to the airport with sufficient time to clear security. Keep in mind that on peak travel days, there will be delays.
- It is the traveler's responsibility to check the airlines web site for delays or changes in flight times. I've been on flights that have left as much as 30 minutes early without any notice from the airline.
- Get spare prescriptions and take them with you on the plane in case you are delayed and separated from your luggage.
- Print your boarding pass 24 hours in advance.
- Make sure you have a confirmed seat assignment.

Avoiding let jag

- Stay well hydrated by drinking plenty of water and avoiding carbonated drinks.
- Eat foods low in sugar and fat content as food is harder to digest at the higher altitudes.
- Dress comfortably and get up and walk around and stretch often.

For international travel

For international travel there is now a new site launched by the US State Department that offers advice, tips for safe travel, country specific information, documentation needed, basically a one stop reference guide. www.studentsabroad.com

➤ Set up 2 free email accounts. If one account doesn't work in one country it could work in another.

➤ Set up skype.

➤ **www.vayama.com** offers information on discount air bargain airfares in Europe.

TIP

PACKING

Essentials that will fit into one 22" suitcase

2 pairs of pants and 2 pairs of shorts
4 shirts and blouses or 4 t-shirts/tank tops
One nice jacket/tie or dress/nice pants and top
Pajamas/nightgown/nightshirt
One turtleneck
Long sleeved shirt
Sweater or fleece
Underwear & socks (no more than a total of 7)
Waterproof jacket, raincoat or foldable
umbrella
Bathing suit
Flip-flops
Dress shoes
Cap/visor
Hairbrush, comb and toothbrush

TIP

Remember, if you take the following items on board a plane, each must be 3 ounces or less and fit into one quart-size bag:

➤ Toothpaste, Deodorant, Shampoo, Conditioner (sometimes provided if staying in hotels, otherwise purchase mini versions)
➤ Contact lens solution
➤ Cosmetics
➤ Shaving cream and razor
➤ Insect repellant/Sunscreen (pack everything in leak-proof plastic bags to contain any spillage)

Wear while traveling

Hooded sweatshirt or sweater

Sneakers/heavy shoes

Packing Tips

- Pack light. Airlines are now charging fees for checked luggage, overweight and oversized bags. Check with your airline for their rules and fees.

  It's so much easier if everything fits into one 22" roll-on bag that you check on international flights and take on domestic flights as carry on. Place a label with your name and address both on the inside and outside of your suitcase. It will make it easier to locate your suitcase should it get lost.
- Don't over pack. You risk losing items if they can't be stuffed back into your luggage after a security check.
- Pack away any removable straps.
- Purchase TSA locks. Use after your flights in the hotels, trains, cabs, etc.
- Make your luggage stand out. Attach a neon tag, ribbon or tape.
- Lighten your load. Make and take along copies of the pages that you'll need from travel guides or textbooks if possible.
- Make a packing list. Keep a copy with you and continue to revise by removing items that you didn't use. If your luggage is lost you'll need a list of its contents for a claim.

- Roll all your clothing. They'll pack easier and wrinkle less.
- Put socks into shoes before packing them. Pack the shoes so that the toe of one shoe is opposite the heel of the other.
- Always place liquids in containers in a plastic bag. A precaution in case of spillage.
- Don't ever pack jewelry in checked luggage.
- Don't forget chargers. Pack phone, computer, iPod chargers, etc.
- Be sure to CARRY medications WITH YOU. Keep in their original containers.
- PACK A CARRY-ON. Be sure to include a change of clothing and toiletries in case your luggage does not arrive at your destination when you do.

CHAPTER

15

Six Little Big Things

▼

CHECKLIST

- ❑ Discuss alcohol and drug use
- ❑ Discuss how to do laundry
- ❑ Demonstrate some basic sewing skills if necessary
- ❑ Discuss the practice of tipping for services rendered

Save more money by:

- Hanging your wet towel to dry and using it more than once.
- Minimize dry cleaning expenses by hanging and taking care of your clothes.

ALCOHOL AND DRUGS

NO MATTER WHAT your experience has been or what your child's expectations are, if you are under 21 consuming alcohol is illegal and using illegal drugs is always illegal.

Your college or university will have a written drug and alcohol policy. It is typically clear and unforgiving. The local police departments also monitor and pay close attention to underage alcohol and drug use and have no problems incarcerating students in jails overnight for their actions. Make sure your student understands this.

Underage drinking is still a problem in colleges. Kate was an EMT and most of her emergency calls were for alcohol poisoning and related problems in college students.

Drinking will not be stopped by policies, but students should begin to understand that as they achieve more freedom and independence, they will assume more responsibility for their own actions.

TIPPING

It's generally a good idea to explain about tipping to your child and the general amount that one is expected to give when rendered an acceptable service.

Food Service

Waiter or counter service	15–20 percent
Buffet	Nothing , however, if someone is refilling your drinks tip the server $1.00–$2.00
Coat check	$1.00 per coat or item

Transportation

Taxi Drivers	15 percent
Airport skycaps	$1.00–$2.00 per bag

CLEANING TIPS

- Line your waste paper baskets . Recycle a plastic grocery shopping bag. It'll be faster to dispose of and you won't have to deal with wet trash due to the extra drops of soda in the can that was thrown away. Better yet, consider recycling cans, cardboard, etc. both in dorm rooms and on campus.
- Buy one all purpose cleaning product.

- Don't throw your wet towels on a pile. The towels will mildew and will not dry. Hang them up.
- Try and keep as little as possible on your dorm room floor.
- Use coasters under cold cans. Any cold container will perspire and get your papers and desk wet.
- Always have a roll of paper towels handy.
- I always use common household bleach to wipe down all the surfaces before I move my children into their dorm rooms—especially the sinks, bathrooms and their floor area. I also use bleach to wash the inside of any rented refrigerator or microwave. Make sure that you have adequate ventilation while doing this and remember to wear gloves and old clothes. Bleach will destroy your clothing and your hands along with the germs.
- Don't ever, ever use a dish liquid detergent (i.e. Dawn, Joy, etc.) in a dishwasher. You will have suds running out of the dishwater onto the floor and everywhere. Some students do not know how to load or use dishwashers. Teach them that dishwashers and washing

machines only function with the detergent made expressly for them and make sure they know how much to use in the dorm or at the laundromat.

LAUNDRY

A Word About Doing Laundry . . .
Remember four things,

1st	Read the garment labels
2nd	Empty all pockets and zip zippers
3rd	Separate clothes into darks and lights
4th	Check all the settings on the machines and make sure they are empty before you put your clothes into them.

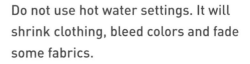

Do not use hot water settings. It will shrink clothing, bleed colors and fade some fabrics.

Leave a laundry basket (with your name on it) on top of the washing machine you're using. Someone can remove your wet laundry and place it into the basket for you in your absence.

➤ Everyone will want to wash their clothes on the weekends. You can expect this to be the busiest time.

➤ A drying rack is helpful to dry delicates and anything that you think might shrink.

Wrinkles

- If you hang your clothes while they are still damp, they will be less wrinkled.
- If you hang your clothes in (a dry location) in the bathroom while a hot shower is on the wrinkles will lessen and possibly completely disappear.
- Shake your clothing and laundry after you take it out of the washer and before you put it into the dryer. You'll have fewer wrinkles to contend with.

MILDEW

Mildew is mold that grows on fabric. Heat and dry air will remove it.

Most often students find mildew in their laundry hampers as a result of throwing their wet towels or sweaty athletic clothing into it and waiting several days to do laundry.

JUST FOR PARENTS

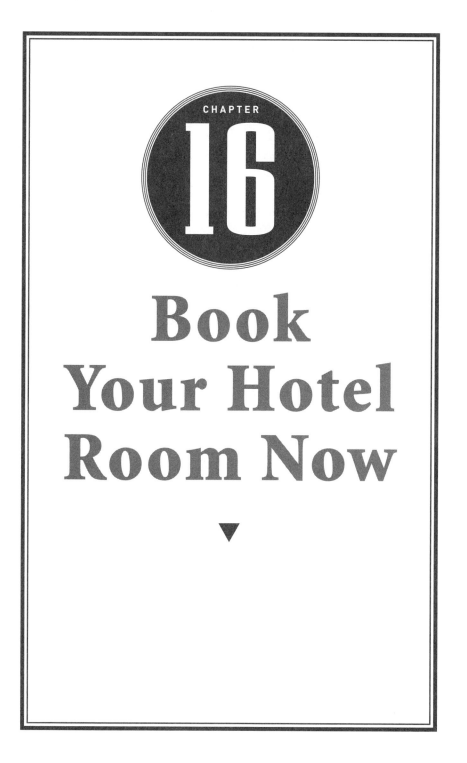

CHAPTER

16

Book Your Hotel Room Now

▼

CHECKLIST

Parents Weekend: _____
- ❏ Hotel reservations made   Confirmation #: _____
- ❏ Travel plans made

Last Day of Classes/Move Out Day: _____
- ❏ Hotel reservations made   Confirmation #: _____
- ❏ Travel plans made

First Day of Next Year/Move In Day: _____
- ❏ Hotel reservations made   Confirmation #: _____
- ❏ Travel plans made

Graduation: _____
- ❏ Hotel reservations made   Confirmation #: _____
- ❏ Travel plans made

OTHER SPECIAL DAYS

Athletic Event: _____
- ❏ Hotel reservations made   Confirmation #: _____
- ❏ Travel plans made

Athletic Event: _____
- ❏ Hotel reservations made   Confirmation #: _____
- ❏ Travel plans made

_____
- ❏ Hotel reservations made   Confirmation #: _____
- ❏ Travel plans made

_____
- ❏ Hotel reservations made   Confirmation #: _____
- ❏ Travel plans made

HOTEL WEBSITES

Best Western	www.bestwestern.com
Candlewood Suites	www.ichotelsgroup.com
Courtyard	www.marriott.com
Crowne Plaza	www.ichotelsgroup.com
Doubletree Hotels	www.doubletree.com
Embassy Suites	www.embassysuites.com
Fairfield Inn	www.marriott.com
Hilton	www.hilton.com
Holiday Inn	www.ichotelsgroup.com
Hotel Indigo	www.ichotelsgroup.com
Hyatt	www.hyatt.com
InterContinental	www.ichotelsgroup.com
Marriott	www.marriott.com
Radisson	www.radisson.com
Ramada	www.ramada.com
Residence Inn	www.marriott.com
Sheraton	www.starwoodhotels.com

Springhill Suites	www.marriott.com
Staybridge Suites	www.ichotelsgroup.com
Westin	www.starwoodhotels.com
Wyndham Hotels	www.wyndham.com

FAVORITE CAMPUS HOTELS

Take the business cards of hotels that you like and tape them here. If business cards aren't available cut off the address and contact information from a piece of stationery or bill.

Hotel Name _____

Address _____

_____

_____

Phone (toll-free) _____

Phone (direct) _____

Parking Available? ❏ YES ❏ NO Cost: _____

PASTE BUSINESS CARD HERE

Inquire as to available parking and costs incurred to use it

Hotel Name _____

Address _____

_____

_____

Phone (toll-free) _____

Phone (direct) _____

Parking Available? ❏ YES ❏ NO Cost: _____

Hotel Name _____

Address _____

_____

_____

Phone (toll-free) _____

Phone (direct) _____

Parking Available? ❏ YES ❏ NO Cost: _____

PASTE BUSINESS CARD HERE

AIRLINES

Airlines		Frequent Flyer #	Pin #
Air Canada	www.aircanada.com 1-888-247-2262		
AirTran	www.airtran.com 1-800-247-8726		
American Airlines	www.aa.com 1-800-433-7300		
American Trans Air	www.ata.com 1-800-225-2995		
British Airways	www.britishairways.com 1-800-247-9297		
Continental Airlines	www.continental.com 1-800-525-0280		
Delta Air Lines	www.delta.com 1-800-221-1212		
JetBlue Airways	www.jetblue.com 1-800-538-2583		
Northwest Airlines	www.nwa.com 1-800-225-2525		
Southwest Airlines	www.southwest.com 1-800-435-9792		
Ted Airlines	www.flyted.com 1-800-225-5833		
United Airlines	www.united.com 1-800-241-6522		
USAir	www.usairways.com 1-800-428-4322		

AUTOMOBILE RENTALS

Company	Website	Phone
Alamo	www.alamo.com	1-800-327-9633
Avis	www.avis.com	1-800-331-1212
Budget	www.budget.com	1-800-527-0700
Dollar	www.dollar.com	1-800-800-4000
Enterprise	www.enterprise.com	1-800-736-8222
Hertz	www.hertz.com	1-800-654-3131
National	www.nationalcar.com	1-800-227-7368
Thrifty	www.thrifty.com	1-800-367-2277

TRAINS

Amtrak
www. amtrak.com • 1-800-523-8720

TAXIS

Company Name _____

Phone Number _____

FAVORITE RESTAURANTS

Name _____

Address _____

Phone _____

Name _____

Address _____

Phone _____

Name _____

Address _____

Phone _____

CHAPTER

17

Kitchen
Table
Connections

▼

CHECKLIST

❑ Address and Phone Number where packages can be sent:

_____

_____

Phone _____

❑ Where Saturday or Sunday next day mail can be sent and
received

_____

_____

Phone _____

❑ Nearest FedEx/Kinko's:

_____

_____

Phone _____

❑ List of Special Occasions

_____

_____

_____

❑ Supplies
  ● Address labels
  ● Boxes
  ● Commercial grade tape
  ● Contents (food, etc.)

MAIL

EVERY CAMPUS UTILIZES a different mail system. Often mail and packages are delivered to a "mail room" and the mail is put into individual student's mail boxes. Notices of special packages that require signatures or are too large for the box, and are kept somewhere else for pick up, will be placed in the mailbox. Often, if a signature is required, your child will need to make arrangements to sign the release before the letter/package can be picked up.

The individual mail boxes are available to the students 24/7 however the mail room, which holds the larger packages and all signature-required items, often is open only during normal business hours.

Most campuses are set up so you can't send items directly to your child's dorm but rather to their mailbox number at the campus mail room.

WARNING

Express Mail/Packages

If you need to get something to your child in a hurry consider other arrangements now, before you need to send something. Keep in mind the facility and the location and hours it will be open for your child to retrieve your package. Many students are in classes when the mail centers are open.

➤ The arrangement that works best for Beth who is at Boston University is to Federal Express any items that she needs instantly from the FedEx/Kinko's in Washington, DC to the FedEx/Kinko's facility on campus. They're open longer hours on the weekends, and are easy walking distance from her room. This allows for the package to be delivered the next day, it's traceable, and Beth can pick it up at her convenience.

➤ Even when I check "no signature required"—it is all too often ignored and my daughters still need to sign.

PACKAGES

Students love to receive mail and packages in addition to text messages and emails. In particular, an unexpected package of goodies from home during the stressful times helps make a student's day. When sending boxes always do it in a fashion that allows you to trace the package should it be lost in transit. Most carriers will send shipment dates and expected delivery confirmations via email to you that can be forwarded to the student. The contents of the boxes that I send are always a surprise, but I inform my daughters of their expected delivery dates.

You'll want to send packages for the following reasons:

1. Most students are without a car and purchasing snack items will be both inconvenient and expensive as they'll be visiting local campus retail establishments.

2. They'll make friends. When packages from home arrive, students share the goodies with all their roommates and friends.

3. You won't want your child to be the only one not receiving a package especially at exam time. There are commercial firms that will be soliciting your business for sending packages to your child. This is your time to shine and provide something bigger and better for less money.

4. It'll give your child a reason to call you. Simply text or email the message "Call me bout pkg u recved" They'll be calling you about "what package?"

When to send packages
- First semester exams
- Second semester exams
- Long holiday weekends that they are spending at school
- Birthdays
- Special award days
- Dates of project or long paper completion
- In honor of academic excellence
- The day before a big athletic competition

Several companies offer you the chance to purchase a series of care packages that they pre-pack and send to your child. You simply place your order for the packages or goodies that you wish for your child to receive in advance along with the desired delivery date. Compare the contents of the packages that these companies offer to send. You can often save money, send more items and have fun doing it yourself.

- At the very least try to send a minimum of three packages during your child's school year.
- For the last five years I have tried to send one package each month to each child. I plan ahead. I get just as much joy out of packing and sending the boxes as my daughters do in receiving them.

Purchasing for packages

You can create wonderful packages at a fraction of the cost if you shop prudently.

1. Purchase large containers of items at the big box warehouse stores or discount stores. Plan on using these goodies in several boxes over several months.
2. Shop the grocery store sales. If granola bars are on sale buy them and save for your next package.
3. Purchase candies and gift items at the after holiday sales.

    I purchase dozens of bags of the green and red foil covered chocolates at the Christmas holiday sales. I separate them into piles of silver foil, red foil and green foil. I use the silver foil covered candies for any box, the red foil covered for the February box (page 217) and the green foil covered for the March box (page 218). Just be sure there aren't any holiday pictures on the candies before you buy them.
4. Plan on purchasing holiday lights when they're on sale.

    I send white lights in December, red lights in February and green lights in March.
5. Plan on purchasing many boxes of brownie mixes, boxes of rice cereal and marshmallows when they're on sale usually in late August and again in November.
6. Many craft stores and general merchandise stores now have bins near

the checkout registers that contain items that sell for 50 cents to one dollar. You can usually find little magnetic frames, soaps, bubble baths, squirt guns, yo-yos etc.

7. The electronic stores have weekly DVD specials. Quite often you can select from dozens of DVDs for $4.99. Around Halloween you can expect to find the "scary movies," and in February the "romances." The Sunday newspaper's circular ads will give you this information. I always have a couple of DVDs on hand in case one of the children is feeling stressed, low in spirits or sick. They're easy to send and sometimes are just what the doctor ordered.

➤ The sale DVDs can be purchased on site in the stores and online. Also, inquire if you can't locate the DVDs that you want in the sale bin there are often more in other locations within the store.

➤ Remember, DVDs can be watched on student laptops.

8. Office supply stores often have school supplies on sale. Highlighters, sticky notepads and index cards are something every student is always in need of.

> I purchase the ink cartridges for my daughters' printers from Quill. The cost of the cartridges is usually sufficient to guarantee free delivery to their dorm and Quill usually has some promotional gift item that is included for free with the purchase. In addition to the ink cartridges my girls have received tool kits, DVDs and candy courtesy of Quill.

A roll of quarters is always welcome for use in vending machines, laundry machines, parking meters, etc.

TIP

SUPPLIES YOU'LL NEED

- **Boxes.** Plan on saving and recycling the boxes that you receive. I prefer to use the Priority Mail Flat Rate Boxes obtained from the United States Post Office. You can order supplies online from www.USPS.com. There are three sizes of flat rate boxes and you can pack as much weight as you can fit into these boxes. You can also pay online, print labels and request a free package pickup.
- Commercial grade tape
- Tissue paper, gift wrap or wax paper

- **Address labels.** Make several labels with your child's address on them at the same time and save the extras noting if it is a post office box or dormitory mail box. This will make a difference in shipping methods. The U.S. Post Office can only receive packages mailed through them.
- **Fillers.** These are the items that you'll want to have on hand to fill in the empty spaces when packing your box:
  - One container of 180 individually wrapped licorice pieces will cost about 4 cents per piece.
  - One box of 24 of the hundred calorie snack packs will cost about 35 cents a piece
  - One box of 60 granola bars will cost about 20 cents each
  - One bag of hard candies will cost about 1 cent each.

Food items

Bagels

Brownies

Candy (in warmer climates avoid chocolates)

Cookies

Crackers

Drink mixes

Dry cereal

Granola bars

Gum

Instant oatmeal and

cereal bowls

Instant soups

Licorice sticks

Marshmallows

Microwave macaroni

and cheese

Nacho chips

Peanut butter

Peanuts and other nuts

Pop tarts

Popcorn (microwave bags)

Raisins

Rice cakes

Salsa

Snack food favorites

Fun items

Bubbles

Desk top games

DVDs

Dorm room survival items:
- 6 in 1 screwdriver,
- travel-size containers

Halloween decorations

Holiday lights and garlands

Inflatable beach ball

Key chains

Magazines

Magnetic frames

Play Doh

Roll of quarters

Rubber duck

Sewing kits

Slinky

Small games

Small puzzle books:

Sudoko, crossword, word search (found in displays near store check-out registers)

Small sized books (3" × 5")

Soaps

Stuffed animal

Squirt guns

Yo-yos

MONTHLY CARE PACKAGES

Each month I send a box that has a theme and is filled with different purchases and home made treats and designed to coincide with a holiday or special occasion. Often these boxes and their contents cost me less than $20.00.

Samples

Not including postage, for less than $10.00 you could send:

- One $4.99 DVD $4.99
- 2 batches of brownies $3.00
  (purchased on sale for $1.50 a box)
- 5 packages of instant ramen noodles $1.00
  (purchased on sale for 20 cents each)

You can add in the following and your care package will be chock full and cost less than $20.00.

- Add in two items found in the $1.00 bin
  $2.00 *(soap, beach ball)*
- 50 licorice sticks $2.00
- 10 granola bars $2.00
- 10 snack packs $3.50

Additional Possible Themes
- All night exam boxes
- Sugar, Sugar, Sugar

September
Occasion/Theme: First Month in College—FUN

Box/Container: Box containing a nalgene water bottle filled with hard candies

Filler: Individually wrapped hard candies and licorice

Toy/Fun Items: Two small $1.00 items and a magazine

Home Bakes Treats: Two batches and/or boxes of brownies, marshmallow crispy rice cereal treats

Food Items: Granola bars, snack packs and instant ramen noodle packages

October
Occasion/Theme: Halloween

Box/Container: Plastic pumpkin or trick or treat bag

Filler: Halloween theme candies (avoid chocolates if shipping to a warm climate)

Toy/Fun Items: Wig, mask, Halloween lights (college students love lights to string around their windows or room) and synthetic spider webs

Home Baked Treats: Crispy rice cereal treats with candy corn on top and cookies

Food Items: Specially marked bags of Halloween pretzels

November

Occasion/Theme: Mid-Semester

Box/Container: Box lined with tissue paper

Filler: Instant hot chocolate packages and tea bags

Toy/Fun Items: Coffee shop gift card and travel coffee mug

Home Baked Treats: Crispy rice cereal treat with fall sugar candies on top and brownies

Food Items: Tea bags—especially herbal and medicinal teas, instant hot chocolate packages, small marshmallows for hot chocolate and packages of microwaveable popcorn

CAUTION

Many hands will be touching your homemade cookies, brownies, etc. Wrap each individually in plastic wrap or in a plastic bag.

Remember allergies—you might need to send gluten free or peanut free boxes.

December
Occasion/Theme: Exam Studying Box

Box/Container: Fun looking tin or plastic container

Filler: Individually wrapped licorice

Toy/Fun Items: Yo-yo, holiday lights, stress reliever ball and stuffed animal

Home Baked Treats: Crispy rice cereal treats with either white/ peppermint chipped chocolate or baking chips on top and brownies

Food Items: Granola bars and lots of different snacks and sweets that will be consumed while studying . . .

- Small packages of cookies, snacks, sweets
- Instant soup packages
- Small containers of tuna fish, cheese and crackers, etc.

- Packages/boxes of instant soups that just need hot water added
- Packages of microwaveable macaroni and cheese
- Packages of microwave popcorn
- Packages of dried fruit

January
Occasion/Theme: Back to School

I usually order a five pound box of fresh oranges/grapefruits to be sent to my daughters from Sun Harvest Citrus: 1-800-743-1480

February
Occasion/Theme: Valentine's Day

Box/Container: Box lined with red tissue paper

Filler: Red foil covered chocolate candies (purchased on sale in December see page 207)

Toy/Fun Items: Package of cute Valentine's day cards, small electronic game, socks, red lights, DVD

Home Baked Treats: Crispy rice cereal treats with cinnamon candies or candy hearts on top

Food Items: Assortment of Valentine candies

March

Occasion/Theme: St. Patrick's Day

Box/Container: Box lined with green tissue paper

Filler: Green foil covered chocolates (purchased on sale in December see page 207)

Toy/Fun Items: Anything for St Patrick's Day—hats, glasses, garland, green lights

Home Baked Treats: Cookies and brownies

Food Items: Soups that are either instant or come in a microwaveable bowl, salt and pepper shakers and a box of crackers

April

Occasion/Theme: Springtime/Beach Related Fun Items

Box/Container: Child's sand bucket with shovel

Filler: Lollipops

Toy/Fun Items: Flip flops, beach balls, squirt guns

Home Baked Treats: Crispy rice cereal treats with chocolate on top

Food Items: Pre-packaged snacks

May

Occasion/Theme: Exam Studying Box

Box/Container: Tin filled with goodies

Filler: Bubble gum, sweets and other snacks

Toy/Fun Items: Send tape, labels and magic markers for boxing items to take back home

Home Baked Treats: Cookies

Food Items: Pre-packaged snacks and popcorn

TIP

➤ College students seem to be impressed with size. I cut the brownies to be at least two inch squares and bag 2–3 cookies at a time.

➤ I've taken an empty box that I wish to fill with goodies with me to the grocery store filling it with goodies as I shopped. After purchasing the items; once home it was easy to refill and ship.

CHAPTER

18

Getting Involved is Good

▼

CHECKLIST

- ❏ Seek out and meet the parent council representatives and volunteers. Offer to help with an event in your home town or to join one of their committees.
- ❏ Reserve hotel rooms now for Parents Weekend
- ❏ Make travel plans now for Parents Weekend
- ❏ Learn how to text message

PARENT COUNCILS AND OTHER VOLUNTEER OPPORTUNITIES

THERE ARE MANY ways parents can be involved in their child's college.
Some examples are:

- Join the parent groups
- Become "college ambassadors" serving as a resource for other parents in the same geographic area
- Host send-off parties in your area for first year students
- Host luncheons for university administrators when they visit your location
- Help the university career center place graduates in new jobs
- Join the development staff and participate in phone-a-thons to encourage fellow parents to support the university

PARENT SUPPORT GROUPS

Empty Nest Support Services

www.emptynestsupport.com is a wonderful resource to help you navigate the road and its challenges while experiencing the empty nest syndrome. It offers a chat room, free newsletter, articles, blogs and much more.

Ask for the brochure "20 Tips for Parents Traveling the Empty Nest Road" by Natalie Caine.

PARENTS WEEKEND

Every college will host a Parent Weekend which is usually one of the most popular weekends of the school year. Family/Parent Weekend gives you the chance to visit with your child and experience life on campus. There is something for everyone with events, activities and programs ranging from lectures and receptions with faculty to performances, jazz brunches and tours. Some colleges let you attend a class and others offer lunch with the students in the dining hall. It's the perfect opportunity for you to see what your child has been doing since you last saw them.

Local hotels book quickly for these weekends. In Texas, Boston and Atlanta I book almost a year in advance. Most of the information and schedules will be posted online and require RSVPs and reservations.

TIP

➤ RSVP early. Often tickets for the musical student productions are sold out quickly.

➤ Confirm a scheduled phone time with your child. For example they will call home every Sunday at 3 P.M.—and if they can't call home then they will notify you and plan an alternate time.

➤ Texas A & M has 126 regional Aggie Mother's Clubs that are an excellent way to support the students while forming friendships and becoming familiar with the university.

TEXT MESSAGING

Learn to text message on your phone. If necessary have your child teach you how to do so. Pre-arrange that they will either call or text when they board planes, arrive at airports, visit friends, etc.

If this is your first time text messaging here are some tips:

- Simplify—be brief with your messages
- Skip as many vowels as you can
- Common abbreviations:
  b   be
  b4   before
  bcus   because

brb	be right back
btw	by the way
CU	see you
Gtg	got to go
hf	have fun
idk	I don't know
imo	in my opinion
jk	just kidding
l8	late
lmao	laughing my a** off
nbd	no big deal
nm	nevermind
noyb	none of your business
np	no problem
omg	Oh my gosh
otl	out to lunch
otoh	on the other hand
pos	parent over shoulder
r	are
re	regarding
ttyl	talk to you later
u	you
w8	wait
w/	with
w/e	whatever
wk	weekend
im	instant messaging
bbm	blackberry messaging

CHAPTER

19

College as a Foreign Language

▼

Academic advisor: Your academic advisor is some one chosen by the university to guide your course selection. You may have a general academic advisor chosen for you when you enter college. However, once you have selected your designated major, you can often request a new academic advisor in your major field.

Academic probation: Occurs when your term or semester GPA falls below a set minimum value, which varies per academic institution. Typically one is expected to meet with counselors and advisors to develop a plan to improve one's GPA by the end of the next semester. If academic performance is not improved by the end of the probation period, expulsion occurs.

Bid: One way of requesting courses is through the bid system. First you need to decide which classes you plan on trying to take the following semester. The next step is to rank these courses—typically the smaller classes, which are harder to get into are given higher preference. Next you allocate your BID points among the courses, with the higher preference given more points. BID points are allocated to each student according to a variety of factors, including your year in college. Seats in classes are given to students according to who placed the most BID points on a selected class. However, students should know that often you have preference in a course in your designated major and as an upperclassman.

Blue light phone: Blue light phones are safety features on college campuses. The blue light indicates that the phone can be used to directly call campus police by pushing the designated button.

Campus police: Each campus has its own police force to help ensure the safety of students and the surrounding community. Students should be aware that campus police can issue parking tickets and other motor vehicle violation tickets. If a student fails to pay tickets issued by the campus police prior to graduation, a student's diploma can be withheld.

Club sports: Club sports are another way for students to get involved on campus. Anyone can join a club sports team and practices are often coordinated by the student members of the club sports team. Teams can compete against other club sports teams and other university teams.

Dual majors: Refers to students who choose to complete two majors during their college career. Students need to make sure that they declare both majors and have the appropriate academic advisors in each field. Your major academic advisors may need to sign off that you have completed the appropriate courses in order to receive your degree.

Freshman fifteen: The freshman fifteen refer to the 15 pounds that some students may gain during their first year of college. However, this can easily be avoided by eating a healthy, well-balanced diet and exercising.

Graduate Student: Refers to any student returning to college to pursue advanced course work.

Greek life: Greek life refers to the fraternities and sororities that are present on a college campus. Greek life also refers to the activities that these Greek organizations coordinate on campus.

GPA: Grade point averages are computed by dividing the number of grade honor points earned by the number of credits.

Hazing: Hazing is the tests and activities that are part of one's initiation into an social organization. Most often people think that hazing occurs in Greek life, however it can occur in any social organization at a university.

Intramural sports: Intramural (IM) sports are university sponsored sports leagues, which are available to any student. However, students are required to register with the IM league as a team and may have to pay a small fee to participate. The IM league then coordinates games and playoffs. Practices are determined by the teams themselves.

Major: A major is your main field of study, for which you will be awarded a degree.

Minor: A minor is another designated field of interest or specialty that you can choose; however, you will not be awarded an additional degree for this course work.

Off campus housing: This term refers to any housing that is not provided by the university.

Pledging: Pledging is the initial period of joining a Greek organization (fraternity or sorority). Pledging often involves learning facts and the history of one's chosen Greek organization and a variety of activities designed to introduce one to the current members of one's Greek organization.

RA: Resident Advisor—is the upperclassman (typically a junior or senior) who is living on your floor in your dorm. RAs often plan various hall or floor activities to help introduce students to each other and also as breaks during the academic year.

Room Draw/Housing Lottery: The housing lottery is the process by which dorm rooms are selected for the next academic year. If you choose to live in university-sponsored housing, you will be randomly assigned a number that designates when you can choose housing. When your number comes up in selection, you can then choose from the available housing. Ways to get around the housing lottery may be requesting block housing (a large portion of rooms in the same location of a dorm) or being "pulled in" to another room. When you are "pulled in," someone who chooses housing before you can also request that you are placed into that dorm option.

Rush: Rush is the period during which Greek organizations select members. During the first round of rush, students visit with several sororities or fraternities of their choice. However, for the subsequent rounds, the

Greek organizations select who is invited back to get to know their organizations. At the end of rush, Greek organizations will extend "bids" to students that they feel would be good matches for their organization. During "bid day" (typically a sorority event) students decide which organization they will join and are welcomed to that organization by its members.

Semester System: The semester system divides the academic year into two portions (semesters), typically September to December and then January to May. Courses last for one semester and one's GPA is determined by end of semester grades.

Student ID: Your student ID is a plastic card, similar to a credit card with your photo and student ID number on the front, and a metallic swipe strip on the back. The swipe strip can function to let you into a variety of university buildings, such as your dorm, the library and cafeterias (based upon your selected meal plan). In addition, students can deposit money onto their student ID card and swipe the card to pay for things on campus, such as coffee, printing and photocopies. Your student ID card is often your ticket into university events and can get you discounts at a variety of places off campus, such as the movie theater.

TA: Teaching Assistant—typically an under-graduate student who has taken the course and done well, or a graduate student who is working with the professor and familiar with the course material. TAs may be assigned to your classes; they can help teach class, run review sessions and may help grade course-work. TAs can be important resources when the professor is not available for course help.

Undergraduate: Refers to any student in college for a bachelor's degree.

CHAPTER

20

Webs Are Not Just for Spiders

▼

ACADEMIC

The internet is an invaluable resource for students.

Newspaper and TV

Great academic resources and will keep students current on daily world events.

www.nytimes.com

www.politico.com

www.washingtonpost.com

Resources

Many college web sites offer free access to journals and magazines. Below are some additional sites to help with those papers.

www.findarticles.com—general article search engine.

---

www.m-w.com—shortened web address for MerriamWebster online dictionary/thesaurus.

www.merriam-webster.com—same as above.

www.Pubmed.com—good scientific journal search webpage. It is a service of the US National Library of Medicine and the National Institutes of Health.

www.sparknotes.com—lists great study guides and online quizzes to help test your knowledge of material.

www.wikipedia.org—Wikipedia, is a "web-based, free content encyclopedia" that allows visitors to list and change information posted for viewers. Note as a result NOT ALL THE INFORMATION POSTED IS CORRECT. This is a site should not be used as a reference or source due to possible discrepancies. Professors have failed students for listing this website as a resource on papers and other projects!

Selecting Courses

These sites allow students to read former students' comments about courses and professors.

www.picaprof.com—view class grade averages and peer reviews about professors and their courses.

www.ratemyprofessors.com—over 1 million professors from 6,000 schools are rated by students.

BOOKS AND TEXTBOOKS

Textbooks are expensive. Here are some alternative ways to procure them at a discount:

Purchasing books online

These sites offer the buyer the ability to purchase books at a discount and the opportunity to resell used books.

www.AbeBooks.com

www.amazon.com

www.bookfinder.com

www.buyusedbooks.com

www.Campusbooks.com

---

www.cheapestbooks.com

www.Ecampus.com

www.half.ebay.com

Swapping or trading books

These are online book swapping sites. Membership (sometimes free) is required to allow one to trade books with other subscribers online.

www.Bookins.com

www.Bookmooch.com

www.Campusbookswap.org—this site run by students acts like a bulletin board giving students an opportunity to buy and sell used textbooks.

www.PaperBackswap.com

www.Traderspress.com

COMMUNICATIONS

Every parent should know about SKYPE.

www.skype.com—this site contains the software (free to download) that allows users to make telephone calls over the internet to other people. You can make free video calls from one PC to another PC anywhere in the world.

E-CARDS

Free electronic cards for all occasions can be found on many sites including these two golden standards.

www.AmericanGreetings.com

www.hallmark.com

ECO-FRIENDLY

Environmentally friendly goods and services allow one to make greener choices. Here are a few sites to help a student "green" their dorm and college life.

www.amazon.com—sells the Bialetti Green Planet pans that are produced with bamboo handles and 50% recycled aluminum.

www.bedbathandbeyond.com—has a complete line of organic cotton and bamboo fiber products.

www.containerstore.com—has eco-friendly organizers for your closet and desk

www.crateandbarrel.com—carries a complete line of bamboo products.

www.ideabite.com—wonderful site full of tips for light-green living.

www.jcpenny.com—in addition to selling organic cotton and bamboo linens, sells bamboo fiber clothing.

www.seventhgeneration.com—creator of environmentally friendly household and personal care products.

www.target.com—target now has over 2,000 eco-friendly items for sale online.

www.walmart.com—carries organic cotton pillows and comforters.

FRIENDSHIP AND PERSONAL

These are social sites that connect people with friends and fellow employees.

www.facebook.com—is the 6th most trafficked site in the US, open to anyone with an email address and a top photo sharing site.

www.myspace.com—social networking site.

FINANCES

Identity theft is one of the fastest growing crimes and 25–35 year olds were most at risk for ID theft last year. Everyone should check their credit report annually.

www.annualcreditreport.com—is the official site to help consumers obtain their free credit report.

Financial aid

Everyone should consider applying for financial aid. Without applying, you won't know if you qualify for grants, scholarships and loan.

www.collegeboard.com

www.fafsa.ed.gov—this site provides eligibility information, electronic filing application form and follow up services for applying for Federal Student Aid

www.finaid.org

www.salliemae.com—site of the nation's leading provider of student loans

www.studentaid.com

GIFTS

Every store has an internet site. Here are 3 of my favorites.

www.1800flowers.com—can provide next day delivery of flowers and other gift items

www.sunharvestcitrus.com—ships Florida citrus fruit

www.thepopcornfactory.com

MUSIC

Here are three popular music downloading sites.

www.itunes.com—offers high quality music that can be downloaded for a nominal fee.

www.Pandora.com—a free online radio website, which allows you to customize your play list by song or artist.

www.YouTube.com—this is a video sharing website. One can upload, view and share video clips.

OFFICE SUPPLIES

Most office supply stores sell online and often offer free shipping.

www.quill.com—Quill Office supplies free shipping on orders over $45.00

www.staples.com

PHOTO SHARING

Every student will be snapping photos, many with their phones. Here are some popular sites.

> **www.facebook.com**—a social network that also is a photo sharing site.

> **www.flickr.com**—one of the best online photo management and sharing sites.

> **www.shutterfly.com**—this site allows you to develop and incorporate your digital prints into many products (cards, albums, photo books) and services.

> **www.webshots.com**—a photo and video sharing site.

SAFETY

In addition to the college campus police, blue lights, and escort service there are organizations that offer advice and course. Such as:

> **www.rainn.org**—202-544-3064 the nation's largest anti-sexual assault organizations.

SEARCH ENGINES

These are web tools designed to help search the internet for information.

www.dogpile.com—searches all the best search engines.

www.google.com

www.vayamu.com—this site searches for the best price on tickets, insurances, etc

search.yahoo.com

SHIPPING

There are many options for shipping items to your students. Speed, cost and weight will often determine which service you choose.

Fedex.kinko.com—a good option for sending something to your child at a location that will be open longer hours than the dorm mail room.

www.ups.com—a cost effective way to ship items. Staples stores offer UPS shipping services.

www.usps—the United States Post office offers 3 different sizes and shapes of flat rate boxes and envelopes. Supplies are free, can be procured online and boxes can't exceed 70 pounds. Good option for shipping books, brownies and other heavy items.

SHOPPING

All major department stores have online websites for shopping and purchasing from all departments.

www.amazon.com

www.ebay.com

www.craigslist.com

www.dormbuys.com

www.overstock.com

SUPPORT GROUPS

If you're feeling lonely and blue, here are two sites just for parents who no longer have children living at home full time.

www.EmptyNestMoms.com

www.EmptyNestSupport.com

TRAVEL

Below are lists of web sites that can ease the planning your next trip

Airlines

www.aircanada.com—Air Canada

---

www.airtran.com—AirTran

www.aa.com—American Airlines

www.ata.com—American Trans Air

www.britishairways.com—British Airways

www.continental.com—Continental Airlines

www.delta.com—Delta Air Lines

www.jetblue.com—JetBlue Airways

www.nwa.com—Northwest Airlines

www.southwest.com—Southwest Airlines

www.flyted.com—Ted Airlines

www.united.com—United Airlines

www.usairways.com—USAir

Hotel Websites

www.bestwestern.com—Best Western

www.ichotelsgroup.com—Candlewood Suites

www.marriott.com—Courtyard

www.ichotelsgroup.com—Crowne Plaza

www.doubletree.com—Doubletree Hotels

www.embassysuites.com—Embassy Suites

www.marriott.com—Fairfield Inn

www.hilton.com—Hilton

www.ichotelsgroup.com—Holiday Inn

www.ichotelsgroup.com—Hotel Indigo

www.hyatt.com—Hyatt

www.ichotelsgroup.com—InterContinental

www.marriott.com—Marriott

www.radisson.com—Radisson

www.ramada.com—Ramada

www.marriott.com—Residence Inn

www.starwoodhotels.com—Sheraton

www.marriott.com—Springhill Suites

www.ichotelsgroup.com—Staybridge Suites

www.starwoodhotels.com—Westin

www.wyndham.com—Wyndham Hotels

International travel

www.studentsabroad.com—provides information and lists resources and tips for students traveling abroad.

www.statravel.com—the largest student travel organization in the world. Students can find and book low cost airfare, rail passes, accommodation, etc They also provide many other products and services such as: the International Student Identity Card and travel insurance.

Packing:

www.OneBag.com—offers advice and details on how to travel light.

www.SmartPacking.com—offers packing light information, airline baggage rules, packing tips, etc.

Tickets and Fares

These comprehensive search engines will help you search for the best price and dates to travel.

www.bookingbuddy.com

www.Expedia.com

www.FareCompare.com—will show the difference in travel dates and prices.

www.independenttraveler.com

www.kayak.com

www.Orbitz.com

www.Travelocity.com

Travel Products

www.eaglecreek.com—leading manufacturer of travel gear.

www.HighSierraSport.com—manufacturer of the carry-on wheeled backpack with removable day pack.

www.minimus.biz—offers thousands of travel size items.

TUTORING

Textbook publishing companies usually list supportive websites that contain practice problems and supplemental chapter notes for each textbook. Simply check inside the front covers to find the listed websites.

Find local tutoring companies that offer group and single tutoring hours.

WEATHER

www.weather.com—good for local weather

Index